THE
BELL CURVE
WARS

THE
BELL CURVE
WARS

Race, Intelligence, and the
Future of America

STEVEN FRASER, EDITOR

BasicBooks
A Division of HarperCollins*Publishers*

Grateful acknowledgment is made for the following:

"Curveball" by Stephen Jay Gould originally appeared in *The New Yorker,* November 28, 1994. Reprinted with permission. © Stephen Jay Gould.

"Cracking Open the IQ Box" by Howard Gardner. Reprinted with permission from *The American Prospect,* Winter 1994. © New Prospect Inc.

"Ethnicity and IQ" by Thomas Sowell. © Thomas Sowell.

Except for chapters by Jacqueline Jones and Orlando Patterson, all other chapters of *The Bell Curve Wars* are expanded versions of articles that appeared in *The New Republic,* October 31, 1994. The original shorter essays of these chapters are copyrighted by *The New Republic.*

Library of Congress Cataloging-in-Publication Data
The bell curve wars : race, intelligence, and the future of America / Steven
  Fraser, editor.
       p.   cm.
    Includes bibliographical references.
    ISBN 0–465–00693–0
    1. Intellect. 2. Nature and nurture. 3. Intelligence levels—United
States. 4. Intelligence levels—United States—Social aspects. 5. Herrn-
stein, Richard J. Bell curve. 6. Educational psychology. I. Fraser,
Steven, 1945–.
BF431.B3749 1995
305.9'082—dc20   95–1880
                                                                  CIP

95 96 97 98 ◆/RRD 9 8 7 6 5 4 3 2 1

Contents

THE
BELL CURVE
WARS

Introduction

Newsweek called it "frightening stuff," worrying that it "may be a mirror for our morally exhausted times," a book that "plays to public anxieties over crime, illegitimacy, welfare dependency, and racial friction." However, contributors to a symposium in *The National Review* described it as "magisterial," and noted that it "confirms ordinary citizens' reasonable intuition that trying to engineer racial equality in the distribution of occupations and social positions runs against not racist prejudice but nature, which shows no such egalitarian distribution of talents." *Time* magazine rejoined by characterizing the book as "845 pages of provocation-with-footnotes," a work of "dubious premises and toxic conclusions." Rushing to the book's defense, the *Wall Street Journal* decried the liberal media for ganging up to excoriate the book, and in particular for engaging in "a frantic race to denounce and destroy Charles Murray" (one of the book's two authors). While *Forbes* applauded the book, and Murray's Jeffersonian vision, *New York Magazine* saw it as "grist for racism of every variety." A columnist for *The New York Times* gloomily concluded: "At least Rush Limbaugh has a sense of humor." Meanwhile, the book was being featured on "Nightline" and showing up on the shelves of K-Marts all over the country.

The Bell Curve: Intelligence and Class Structure in American Life by Richard J. Herrnstein and Charles Murray is clearly the most incendiary piece of social science to appear in the last decade or more. It's easy to understand why. *The Bell Curve* irritates every abraded nerve in our public consciousness about race and social class. In form it is practically a model of academic etiquette, sober not inflammatory in style, dutifully acknowledging contrary views, encasing its own viewpoint in a thick statistical armature. But despite the hedgerows of caveats and equivocations with which the authors surround their most provocative claims, *The Bell Curve* is an explosive device. Its premises, its purported findings, its prescriptive advice for what ails American society are—whether or not the authors deliberately designed them to be so—shocking.

There is, for example, the book's hubris; the clear implication that it constitutes a kind of Rosetta stone with which to decipher in one fell swoop all of the country's social pathologies. Once we correctly understand the role of statistically measured intelligence, the inexorable logic of the social arithmetic that sorts us out into rich and poor, powerful and powerless, will become blindingly apparent. The authors assure us we will no longer "grope with symptoms instead of causes" or "stumble into supposed remedies that have no chance of working."

It is hard to recall when there last appeared a work of such daunting omniscience, one offering such presumptuous single-minded wisdom. Many of the most painful dilemmas afflicting our society, when viewed through the prism of *The Bell Curve*, seem if not remediable then at least cleansed of their bewildering complexity. Low intelligence lurks in the shadows of "irresponsible child-rearing and parenting behavior." It looms again as "a cause of unemployment and poverty." Indeed, not only poverty and unemployment but crime, unwed motherhood, school failure, workplace accidents, welfare dependency, and broken families emerge demonically out of the Pandora's box of sub-par IQ scores. This news about our social afflictions is terrible, but the simple elegance of the authors' diagnosis is nonetheless intellectually stunning.

Then there is the book's profound fatalism and austere elitism, both so extraordinary in a habitually optimistic and democratically inclined nation. If group differences in intelligence are to some large degree hereditary and therefore intractable, and if we have become a hierarchical society, polarized into an empowered "cognitive elite" at the top and a sociopathic "cognitive underclass" at the bottom— a hierarchy that merely replicates an ascending slope of IQ scores— then, the authors feel obligated to tell us, public policy stands helpless to do anything about it: thus, "success and failure in the American economy, and all that goes with it, are increasingly a matter of the genes that people inherit," and "programs to expand opportunities for the disadvantaged are not going to make much difference." Grim pronouncements indeed. Inequality, inequality of the most fundamental sort, is our inexorable fate however much the nation's democratic and egalitarian credo might groan in protest.

Yet alongside this air of fatalistic resignation, Murray and Herrnstein convey an equally astonishing sense of activism and missionary purpose, which also helps account for the book's remarkable notoriety. They worry about "dysgenesis," or what others have less elegantly characterized as the "dumbing-down of America," due to the higher fertility rates of the "cognitive underclass." Here the authors are more sanguine about the efficacy of public policy, suggesting, albeit with some tentativeness, given the extreme delicacy of the subject, that changes in immigration law and welfare and public health reforms targeted particularly at unwed mothers might arrest the genetic degradation of the national stock. Not since the eugenics craze of the 1920s has this line of thought occupied a serious place on the national agenda.

Numerous other claims and assertions have generated flash floods of letters to the editor in every major magazine and newspaper, not to mention over-the-air commentary on scores of radio and television shows. For example, the authors' insistence on the predominance of our genetic make-up over environmental factors in determining how well we do on an IQ test stirs controversy; so too, their presumption that "intelligence," or what some psychometricians call g, is a uniform, quantifiable power measurable across differences in history, culture, and environment. All of these issues and more are examined in the essays that follow.

But above all, of course, it is what *The Bell Curve* says, or at least seems to say—notwithstanding disclaimers by the authors in and outside of the text—about race, intelligence, and social hierarchy that has ignited the media firestorm. In a country necessarily preoccupied throughout its whole history with race relations, the book's claim to offer scientific proof of the inferiority of black people was bound to eclipse all its other possible subjects in public debate. The authors demur, noting that there's hardly a word about race—or rather that the book is only about the "white race"—until chapter 13, more than halfway through the main body of the text. More to the point, the subtitle of the book says it's about "intelligence and class structure in American life," not about intelligence and race. In some sense the authors are quite right. The book is indeed about class in America, a stark fact noteworthy in its own right. However, *The Bell Curve* colors the class structure in unmistakable shades of black and white, neutralizing simmering tensions over economic inequality with highly charged notions of race phobia and inferiority.

Words like "class" and phrases like "class structure" are rarely heard nowadays. To suddenly see them blazoned across the jacket of a best-selling book by two conservative social scientists is therefore especially striking. Yet for well over a century, from the age of Jackson through the age of FDR, such words were a common enough part of our national vocabulary. Usually they were deployed to signal serious maldistributions of power and wealth and often carried with them a moral opprobrium directed at landed, industrial, or financial elites. Then, sometime after World War II, questions of class inequalities lost their urgency, subsided, and even vanished from the public arena. To watch them resurface in the pages of *The Bell Curve* is a bracing reminder that the abrasions of social class remain an abiding reality for Americans, whether they are mirrored in popular rhetoric or not. More than that, however, the "class struggle," as retold in *The Bell Curve*, marks a seismic shift in the moral valence of the idea of class in American life.

If at one time, examining the nation's class structure implicitly called into question the moral legitimacy, democratic commitments, and economic fairness of the country's most powerful institutions and wealthiest individuals, *The Bell Curve* is telling us that the shoe is now very much on the other foot. While the authors lament the social isolation of the "cognitive elite," walled off from the rest of society in its privileged compounds, the brunt of the book is about the transgressions of the lower orders, cognitive or otherwise. At a time when most indices record expanding inequalities in American life—not only in income and wealth distribution, but in public and private schooling, in matters of health care, even in our varying capacities to rear the newborn—*The Bell Curve* naturalizes those phenomena, turns them into inescapable symptoms of a biological class fate. At the same time, by associating the "cognitive underclass" with every grisly or disturbing form of social behavior, from crime to unwed teenage motherhood, the authors direct our gaze away from those institutional centers of power that in an earlier era might have had to shoulder the blame for our most grievous inequalities and social pathologies.

Once a way of interrogating the powerful, in the hands of Murray and Herrnstein, the study of "class structure" has become instead an implicit indictment of the powerless, the "scientific" rationale others may use to find them blameworthy and to prepare some condign punishment. This too helps account for the book's renown. It allows for discussion of the vexed issue of social inequality at a moment when the hierarchies of American life grow more distended and rigid; but it lets the anxieties and resentments naturally aroused by those developments flow downward toward a defenseless "cognitive underclass." The fact that that class turns out to be disproportionately black is undoubtedly an important political and psychological consolation for some—and it severely weakens the authors' contention that their book is not about race. Still, *The Bell Curve*'s distinctive class agenda is made unmistakably clear when the reader is reminded that "the high rates of poverty that afflict certain segments of the white population are determined more by intelligence than by socioeconomic background."

The Bell Curve Wars: Race, Intelligence, and the Future of America responds to these and other vital issues raised by the Murray and Herrnstein book. There is no neat way to pigeonhole the essays that follow. Some criticize *The Bell Curve*'s premises regarding genetics, the nature of human intelligence, and the very concept of race. Some dispute its statistical methods and findings or the credibility of its sources. Others question its depiction of America's "class structure" or the book's policy recommendations. Several speculate about the remarkable public reaction to the book. A few do a bit of everything. Taken together they comprise a powerful antidote to a work of dubious premises and socially alarming predictions.

As Stephen Jay Gould once took on Herrnstein and Murray's predecessors in his book *The Mismeasure of Man,* so here he attacks *The Bell Curve*'s scientific pretensions as he dismantles its four most basic premises regarding intelligence and genetics: that intelligence can be described by a single number; that it is capable of ranking people in some linear order; that it is genetically based; and that it is immutable. Cognitive psychologist Howard Gardner questions the scientific underpinnings of *The Bell Curve* by noting that it ignores the past 100 years of biological, psychological, and anthropological research that challenges the notion of a single, uniform, and innate human intelligence, or *g*. He argues instead for the concept of "multiple intelligences"—practical, social, musical, spatial, and so on—and for the enormously important but underrated role of training in the attainment of any kind of intelligence. The scientific assault is joined from yet another quarter by the eminent psychometrician Richard Nisbett. Based on his painstaking examination of all the existing serious scientific studies of intelligence, Nisbett finds that most point to a zero genetic contribution to the black-white differential in IQ. He concludes that Murray and Herrnstein's slipshod treatment of this and other vital statistical questions would prohibit their publication in any respectable peer-reviewed journal. *New Republic* editors Jeffrey Rosen and Charles Lane question the integrity of the book's scholarly infrastructure. Scrutinizing *The Bell Curve*'s footnotes and bibliography, Rosen and Lane conclude that the authors have in effect synthesized the work of "disreputable race theorists and eccentric eugenicists" in mounting some of their key arguments. Dante Ramos of *The New Republic* similarly comments that there is "too much counter-evidence relegated to endnotes, too much tendentious data interpretation, and too many not-quite-credible studies."

A number of commentators have questioned the book's historical nearsightedness; for example, its conspicuous failure to explain the long-term decline in poverty during the reign of the welfare state (roughly from 1940 to 1970). In his essay here, Thomas Sowell, conservative intellectual and *Forbes* magazine columnist, challenges the authors' claims about the genetic basis for ethnic group differences in intelligence by appealing to the historical record. He points out that the relative performance of various ethnic groups on intelligence tests has changed greatly over time, and that these ethnic groups have dramatically shifted position on the IQ ladder even while their rates of intermarriage remained low and unchanged. This has been true not only of Ashkenazi Jews (the most favored "race" within Murray and Herrnstein's "cognitive elite"), but of Poles and Italians as well. Jacqueline Jones, historian of the working poor, both black and white, argues that *The Bell Curve* is only "the most recent in a long line of efforts to prove the congenital inferiority of poor people in general. . . and black people in particular." Her essay is an eye-opening comparison of *The Bell Curve* with those now long-forgotten justifications of slavery and segregation that rested on the alleged mental inferiority of African Americans. Henry Louis Gates, Jr., W. E. B. Du Bois Professor of the Humanities at Harvard, unearths an apposite observation by Frederick Douglass that reminds us of the creative labors of past master classes seeking some justification for their domination in the failings of those they dominated. Gates notes that *The Bell Curve* appears at a moment in our history when its behavioral explanation for the persisting misery of our inner cities sits well with an electorate, and especially a Congress, deeply reluctant to commit substantial resources toward the eradication of poverty.

Andrew Hacker, author of *Two Nations: Black and White, Separate, Hostile, Unequal,* and Alan Wolfe, author of several books on American intellectual life, challenge *The Bell Curve*'s version of today's class structure. Rejecting the book's thesis that the sort of verbal virtuosity or expertise at abstraction that tends to show up well on IQ tests is the equivalent of intelligence, Hacker denies that a caste of high test scorers or "testocracy" dominates our society. He furthermore asks why Murray and Herrnstein fail to analyze the criminal behavior of the white collar "cognitive elite" (which after all entails a very substantial financial burden on the rest of us), speculating that the authors' social prejudice leads them to treat their crimes as less menacing "because their commission calls for brains rather than brawn." Alan Wolfe, who calls *The Bell Curve* a "*Communist Manifesto* for the mind," shows that the book's attempt to prove there has been a revolution in the country's class structure falls apart upon close inspection. Wolfe maintains that there's no evidence of a relationship between test scores, even at the best colleges, and later career success, and no hard linkage between IQ and job performance; nor does IQ predict income disparities later in life. John Judis, who writes about

American culture and intellectual history, notes that for a book ostensibly about the recent and alarming growth in disparities of income, wealth, and standard of living, *The Bell Curve* is remarkably silent about such clearly relevant considerations as the decline of trade unions, the out-sourcing of manufacturing, the growth of foreign competition, and so on.

Judis is even more upset, as are a number of other contributors, with the book's implications for public policy. He homes in on the authors' evasiveness, showing that despite public denials by Murray, *The Bell Curve* builds a brief on behalf of eugenics and the continued rule of the "cognitive elite." Mickey Kaus, author of *The End of Equality,* is disturbed by the harsh vision of America, appearing near the end of *The Bell Curve,* in which the "cognitive underclass" ends up consigned to the stern ministrations of a "custodial state." Citing an avalanche of evidence suggesting the environmental basis of ethnic differences in intelligence, Kaus concludes that, in contrast to *The Bell Curve*'s relentless attack on most meliorative measures, there's every reason to believe improving the awful environment in which many black children grow up will markedly close *The Bell Curve* gap. So, too, the esteemed social scientist Nathan Glazer, while more agnostic about the underlying reasons for IQ differences, laments the book's "quietism regarding our greatest social problem" when there's still so much that could be attempted to remedy the plight of African Americans.

A number of the contributions to *The Bell Curve Wars* express the moral forebodings conjured up by a book so at odds with the nation's democratic and egalitarian faith. Martin Peretz, publisher of *The New Republic,* muses about the book's alarming reverberations in a country that sometimes seems all too much in a hurry to forsake its historic belief in equality. Leon Wieseltier, the literary editor of *The New Republic* (whose essay is a response to an article by Murray and Herrnstein appearing in that magazine) refuses to grant some privileged status to the authors' putative "science" or to credit their portrait of themselves as heroic venturers into the intellectual unknown. Instead, he characterizes their views as "old, dreary and indecent, philosophically shabby and politically ugly," and argues that the determinism and materialism of the Murray and

Herrnstein position are at odds with the American credo of individual freedom.

Wieseltier strikes a personal note, remarking on the significance of his own Jewish origins in the Herrnstein-Murray view of the world. Hugh Pearson, the biographer of Huey Newton, does something similar. While he deplores much about *The Bell Curve*, he doesn't want African Americans to use it as a psychological crutch, a justification "to continue viewing ourselves as victims," clinging to "old standards" and "old solutions."

Public reaction to the book is very much on the minds of other contributors as well. Michael Lind, an editor at *Harper's* magazine, is particularly intrigued by the "sudden and astonishing legitimation, by the leading intellectuals and journalists of the mainstream American right, of a body of racialist pseudoscience." His essay explores the recent transformation of the conservative movement that now embraces an outlook that, even through the Reagan years, was repudiated by the intellectually responsible right wing.

Randall Kennedy of the Harvard Law School is deeply worried about the enormous hype surrounding the publication of *The Bell Curve* as well as its acceptance by important arbiters of public opinion as "within the pale of respectable discussion," despite its conspicuous deficiencies and its defamation of African Americans. Such a triumph lends great credence to a long tradition of pessimism about the future of race relations in America. Kennedy probes the mores of the mass media to help explain how a book avowing a theory of black inferiority achieved such legitimacy.

Orlando Patterson, author of *Freedom*, concludes with an essay that ranges widely across much of the treacherous scientific and sociological terrain covered by *The Bell Curve*. Along the way, he asks a fundamental question raised by the book's success: "Why is it that, in a land founded on the secular belief that 'all men are created equal,' we are so obsessed with the need to find a scientific basis for human inequality?"—an obsession that invariably seems directed at African Americans. Patterson notes, for example, that although there are clear regional variations between rural white Southerners and their Northern urban counterparts in measured IQ as well as in cultural and economic performance, no one has ever sounded a national alarm bell about these differences, except in the most sympathetic tones. While we do not neglect such discrepancies, we do not make them the occasion for "wantonly insulting and dishonoring these people." The reason is both obvious and chilling. If rural white people are considered members in good standing of the nation's social and moral community, black people are forever on probation. Professor Patterson's essay probes the reasons why.

The Bell Curve Wars does not pretend to offer a unified viewpoint. Its contributors have varying estimations of the book they were assembled to write about. But even the most conservative among them find themselves disturbed; either by one or several of its more suspect premises or conclusions, or by what the extraordinary reception accorded *The Bell Curve* might portend for our society. Inescapably, one must wonder whether its ubiquitous presence serves to validate—through its voluminous pages, its social scientese, its panoply of graphs, charts, and appendices—feelings deeply buried in our society about the inferiority of African Americans, feelings that have in recent years once again bubbled to the surface. What *The Bell Curve Wars* hopes to provide is a multifaceted challenge to a book whose prognosis for the future of America could hardly be grimmer.

STEVEN FRASER

Curveball

STEPHEN JAY GOULD

The Bell Curve, by Richard J. Herrnstein and Charles Murray (Free Press; $30), subtitled *Intelligence and Class Structure in American Life,* provides a superb and unusual opportunity to gain insight into the meaning of experiment as a method in science. The primary desideratum in all experiments is reduction of confusing variables: we bring all the buzzing and blooming confusion of the external world into our laboratories and, holding all else constant in our artificial simplicity, try to vary just one potential factor at a time. But many subjects defy the use of such an experimental method—particularly most social phenomena—because importation into the laboratory destroys the subject of the investigation, and then we must yearn for simplifying guides in nature. If the external world occasionally obliges by holding some crucial factors constant for us, we can only offer thanks for this natural boost to understanding.

So, when a book garners as much attention as *The Bell Curve,* we wish to know the causes. One might suspect the content itself—a startlingly new idea, or an old suspicion newly verified by persuasive data—but the reason might also be social acceptability, or even just plain hype. *The Bell Curve,* with its claims and supposed documentation that race and class differences are largely caused by genetic factors and are therefore essentially immutable, contains no new arguments and presents no compelling data to support its anachronistic social Darwinism, so I can only conclude that its success in winning attention must reflect the depressing temper of our time—a historical moment of unprecedented ungenerosity, when a mood for slashing social programs can be powerfully abetted by an argument that beneficiaries cannot be helped, owing to inborn cognitive limits expressed as low IQ scores.

The Bell Curve rests on two distinctly different but sequential arguments, which together encompass the classic corpus of biological determinism as a social philosophy. The first argument rehashes the tenets of social Darwinism as it was originally constituted. "Social Darwinism" has often been used as a general term for any evolutionary argument about the biological basis of human differences, but the initial nineteenth-century meaning referred to a specific theory of class stratification within industrial societies, and particularly to the idea that there was a permanently poor underclass consisting of genetically inferior people who had precipitated down into their inevitable fate. The theory arose from a paradox of egalitarianism: as long as people remain on top of the social heap by accident of a noble name or parental wealth, and as long as members of despised castes cannot rise no matter what their talents, social stratification will not reflect intellectual merit, and brilliance will be distributed across all classes; but when true equality of opportunity is attained smart people rise and the lower classes become rigid, retaining only the intellectually incompetent.

This argument has attracted a variety of twentieth-century champions, including the Stanford psychologist Lewis M. Terman, who imported Alfred Binet's original test from France, developed the Stanford-Binet IQ test, and gave a hereditarian interpretation to the results (one that Binet had vigorously rejected in developing this style of test); Prime Minister Lee Kuan Yew of Singapore, who tried to institute a eugenics program of rewarding well-educated women for higher birth rates; and Richard Herrnstein, a co-author of *The Bell Curve* and also the author of a 1971 *Atlantic Monthly* article that presented the same argument without the documentation. The general claim is neither uninteresting nor illogical, but it does require the validity of four shaky premises, all asserted (but hardly discussed or defended) by Herrnstein and Murray. Intelligence, in their formulation, must be depictable as a single number, capable of ranking people in linear order, genetically based, and effectively immutable. If any of these premises are false, their entire argument collapses. For example, if all are true except immutability, then programs for early intervention in education might work to boost IQ permanently, just as a pair of eyeglasses may correct a genetic defect in vision. The central argument of *The Bell Curve* fails because most of the premises are false.

Herrnstein and Murray's second claim, the lightning rod for most commentary, extends the argument for innate cognitive stratification to a claim that racial differences in IQ are mostly determined by genetic causes—small difference for Asian superiority over Caucasian, but large for Caucasians over people of African descent. This argument is as old as the study of race, and is most surely fallacious. The last generation's discussion centered on Arthur Jensen's 1980 book *Bias in Mental Testing* (far more elaborate and varied than anything presented in *The Bell Curve,* and therefore still a better source for grasping the argument and its problems), and on the cranky advocacy of William Shockley, a Nobel Prize–winning physicist. The central fallacy in using the substantial heritability of within-group IQ (among whites, for example) as an explanation of average differences between groups (whites versus blacks, for example) is now well known and acknowledged by all, including Herrnstein and Murray, but deserves a restatement by example. Take a trait that is far more heritable than anyone has ever claimed IQ to be but is politically uncontroversial—body height. Suppose that I measured the heights of adult males in a poor Indian village beset with nutritional deprivation, and suppose the average height of adult males is five feet six inches. Heritability within the village is high, which is to say that tall fathers (they may average five feet eight inches) tend to have tall sons, while short fathers (five feet four inches on average) tend to have short sons. But this high heritability within the village does not mean that better nutrition might not raise average height to five feet ten inches in a few generations. Similarly, the well-documented fifteen-point average difference in IQ between blacks and whites in America, with substantial heritability of IQ in family lines within each group, permits no automatic conclusion that truly equal opportunity might not raise the black average enough to equal or surpass the white mean.

Disturbing as I find the anachronism of *The Bell Curve,* I am even more distressed by its pervasive disingenuousness. The authors omit facts, misuse statistical methods, and seem unwilling to admit the consequences of their own words.

The ocean of publicity that has engulfed *The Bell Curve* has a basis in what Murray and Herrnstein, in an article in *The New Republic* last month [Oct. 31, 1994], call "the flashpoint of intelligence as a public topic: the question of genetic differences between the races." And yet, since the day of the book's publication, Murray (Herrnstein died a month before the book appeared) has been temporizing, and denying that race is an important subject in the book at all; he blames the press for unfairly fanning these particular flames. In *The New Republic* he and Herrnstein wrote, "Here is what we hope will be our contribution to the discussion. We put it in italics; if we could, we would put it in neon lights: *The answer doesn't much matter.*"

Fair enough, in the narrow sense that any individual may be a rarely brilliant member of an averagely dumb group (and therefore not subject to judgment by the group mean), but Murray cannot deny that *The Bell Curve* treats race as one of two major topics, with each given about equal space; nor can he pretend that strongly stated claims about group differences have no political impact in a society obsessed with the meanings and consequences of ethnicity. The very first sentence of *The Bell Curve*'s preface acknowledges that the book treats the two subjects equally: "This book is about differences in intellectual capacity among people and groups and what those differences mean for America's future." And Murray and Herrnstein's *New Republic* article begins by identifying racial differences as the key subject of interest: "The private dialogue about race in America is far different from the public one."

Furthermore, Herrnstein and Murray know and acknowledge the critique of extending the substantial heritability of within-group IQ to explain differences between groups, so they must construct an admittedly circumstantial case for attributing most of the black-white mean difference to irrevocable genetics—while properly stressing that the average difference doesn't help in judging any particular person, because so many individual blacks score above the white mean in IQ. Quite apart from the rhetoric dubiety of this old ploy in a shopworn genre—"Some of my best friends are Group X"—Herrnstein and Murray violate fairness by converting a complex case that can yield only agnosticism into a biased brief for permanent and heritable difference. They impose this spin by turning every straw on their side into an oak, while mentioning but downplaying the strong circumstantial case for substantial malleability and little average genetic difference. This case includes such evidence as impressive IQ scores for poor black children adopted into affluent and intellectual homes; average IQ increases in some nations since the Second World War equal to the entire fifteen-point difference now separating blacks and whites in America; and failure to find any cognitive differences between two cohorts of children born out of wedlock to German women, reared in Germany as Germans, but fathered by black and white American soldiers.

The Bell Curve is even more disingenuous in its argument than in its obfuscation about race. The book is a rhetorical masterpiece of scientism, and it benefits from the particular kind of fear that numbers impose on nonprofessional commentators. It runs to 845 pages, including more than a hundred pages of appendixes filled with figures. So their text looks complicated, and reviewers shy away with a knee-jerk claim that, while they suspect fallacies of argument, they really cannot judge. In the same issue of *The New Republic* as Murray and Herrnstein's article, Mickey Kaus writes, "As a lay reader of 'The Bell Curve,' I am unable to judge fairly," and Leon Wieseltier adds, "Murray, too, is hiding the hardness of his politics behind the hardness of his science. And his science, for all I know, is soft. . . . Or so I imagine. I am not a scientist. I know nothing about psychometrics." And Peter Passell, in the *Times:* "But this reviewer is not a biologist, and will leave the argument to experts."

    The book is in fact extraordinarily one-dimensional. It makes no attempt to survey the range of available data, and pays astonishingly little attention to the rich and informative history of its contentious subject. (One can only recall Santayana's dictum, now a cliché of intellectual life: "Those who cannot remember the past are condemned to repeat it.") Virtually all the analysis rests on a single technique applied to a single set of data—probably done in one computer run. (I do agree that the authors have used more appropriate technique and the best source of information. Still, claims as broad as those advanced in *The Bell Curve* simply cannot be properly defended—that is, either supported or denied—by such a restricted approach.) The blatant errors and inadequacies of *The Bell Curve* could be picked up by lay reviewers if only they would not let themselves be frightened by numbers—for Herrnstein and Murray do write clearly, and their mistakes are both patent and accessible.

While disclaiming his own ability to judge, Mickey Kaus, in *The New Republic,* does correctly identify the authors' first two claims that are absolutely essential "to make the pessimistic 'ethnic difference' argument work": "1) that there is a single, general measure of mental ability; 2) that the IQ tests that purport to measure this ability. . . aren't culturally biased."

Nothing in *The Bell Curve* angered me more than the authors' failure to supply any justification for their central claim, the sine qua non of their entire argument: that the number known as *g*, the celebrated "general factor" of intelligence, first identified by the British psychologist Charles Spearman, in 1904, captures a real property in the head. Murray and Herrnstein simply declare that the issue has been decided, as in this passage from their *New Republic* article: "Among the experts, it is by now beyond much technical dispute that there is such a thing as a general factor of cognitive ability on which human beings differ and that this general factor is measured reasonably well by a variety of standardized tests, best of all by IQ tests designed for that purpose." Such a statement represents extraordinary obfuscation, achievable only if one takes "expert" to mean "that group of psychometricians working in the tradition of *g* and its avatar IQ" The authors even admit that there are three major schools of psychometric interpretation and that only one supports their view of *g* and IQ.

But this issue cannot be decided, or even understood, without discussing the key and only rationale that has maintained *g* since Spearman invented it: factor analysis. The fact that Herrnstein and Murray barely mention the factor-analytic argument forms a central indictment of *The Bell Curve* and is an illustration of its vacuousness. How can the authors base an 800-page book on a claim for the reality of IQ as measuring a genuine, and largely genetic, general cognitive ability—and then hardly discuss, either pro or con, the theoretical basis for their certainty?

Admittedly, factor analysis is a difficult mathematical subject, but it can be explained to lay readers with a geometrical formulation developed by L. L. Thurstone, an American psychologist, in the 1930s and used by me in a full chapter on factor analysis in my 1981 book *The Mismeasure of Man*. A few paragraphs cannot suffice for adequate explanation, so, although I offer some sketchy hints below, readers should not question their own IQs if the topic still seems arcane.

In brief, a person's performance on various mental tests tends to be positively correlated—that is, if you do well on one kind of test, you tend to do well on the other kinds. This is scarcely surprising, and is subject to interpretation that is either purely genetic (that an innate thing in the head boosts all performances) or purely environmental (that good books and good childhood nutrition boost all performances); the positive correlations in themselves say nothing about causes. The results of these tests can be plotted on a multidimensional graph with an axis for each test. Spearman used factor analysis to find a single dimension—which he called g—that best identifies the common factor behind positive correlations among the tests. But Thurstone later showed that g could be made to disappear by simply rotating the dimensions to different positions. In one rotation Thurstone placed the dimensions near the most widely separated attributes among the tests, thus giving rise to the theory of multiple intelligences (verbal, mathematical, spatial, etc., with no overarching g). This theory (which I support) has been advocated by many prominent psychometricians, including J. P. Guilford, in the 1950s, and Howard Gardner today. In this perspective g cannot have inherent reality, for it emerges in one form of mathematical representation for correlations among tests and disappears (or greatly attenuates) in other forms, which are entirely equivalent in amount of information explained. In any case, you can't grasp the issue at all without a clear exposition of factor analysis—and *The Bell Curve* cops out on this central concept.

As for Kaus's second issue, cultural bias, the presentation of it in *The Bell Curve* matches Arthur Jensen's and that of other hereditarians, in confusing a technical (and proper) meaning of "bias" (I call it "S-bias," for "statistical") with the entirely different vernacular concept (I call it "V-bias") that provokes popular debate. All these authors swear up and down (and I agree with them completely) that the tests are not biased—in the statistician's definition. Lack of S-bias means that the same score, when it is achieved by members of different groups, predicts the same thing; that is, a black person and a white person with identical scores will have the same probabilities for doing anything that IQ is supposed to predict.

But V-bias, the source of public concern, embodies an entirely different issue, which, unfortunately, uses the same word. The public wants to know whether blacks average 85 and whites 100 because society treats blacks unfairly—that is, whether lower black scores record biases in this social sense. And this crucial question (to which we do not know the answer) cannot be addressed by a demonstration that S-bias doesn't exist, which is the only issue analyzed, however correctly, in *The Bell Curve*.

The book is also suspect in its use of statistics. As I mentioned, virtually all its data derive from one analysis—a plotting, by a technique called multiple regression, of social behaviors that agitate us, such as crime, unemployment, and births out of wedlock (known as dependent variables), against both IQ and parental sociometric status (known as independent variables). The authors first hold IQ constant and consider the relationship of social behaviors to parental socioeconomic status. They then hold socioeconomic status constant and consider the relationship of the same social behaviors to IQ. In general, they find a higher correlation with IQ than with socioeconomic status; for example, people with low IQ are more likely to drop out of high school than people whose parents have low socioeconomic status.

But such analyses must engage two issues—the form and the strength of the relationship—and Herrnstein and Murray discuss only the issue that seems to support their viewpoint, while virtually ignoring (and in one key passage almost willfully hiding) the other.

Their numerous graphs present only the form of the relationships; that is, they draw the regression curves of their variables against IQ and parental socioeconomic status. But, in violation of all statistical norms that I've ever learned, they plot only the regression curve and do not show the scatter of variation around the curve, so their graphs do not show anything about the strength of the relationships—that is, the amount of variation in social factors explained by IQ and socioeconomic status. Indeed, almost all their relationships are weak: very little of the variation in social factors is explained by either independent variable (though the form of this small amount of explanation does lie in their favored direction). In short, their own data indicate that IQ is not a major factor in determining variation in nearly all the social behaviors they study—and so their conclusions collapse, or at least become so greatly attenuated that their pessimism and conservative social agenda gain no significant support.

Herrnstein and Murray actually admit as much in one crucial passage, but then they hide the pattern. They write, "It [cognitive ability] almost always explains less than 20 percent of the variance, to use the statistician's term, usually less than 10 percent and often less than 5 percent. What this means in English is that you cannot predict what a given person will do from his IQ score. . . . On the other hand, despite the low association at the individual level, large differences in social behavior separate groups of people when the groups differ intellectually on the average." Despite this disclaimer, their remarkable next sentence makes a strong causal claim. "We will argue that intelligence itself, not just its correlation with socioeconomic status, is responsible for these group differences." But a few percent of statistical determination is not causal explanation. And the case is even worse for their key genetic argument, since they claim a heritability of about 60 percent for IQ, so to isolate the strength of genetic determination by Herrnstein and Murray's own criteria you must nearly halve even the few percent they claim to explain.

My charge of disingenuousness receives its strongest affirmation in a sentence tucked away on the first page of Appendix 4, page 593. the authors state, "In the text, we do not refer to the usual measure of goodness of fit for multiple regressions, R^2, but they are presented here for the cross-sectional analyses." Now, why would they exclude from the text, and relegate to an appendix that very few people will read, or even consult, a number that, by their own admission, is "the usual measure of goodness of fit"? I can only conclude that they did not choose to admit in the main text the extreme weakness of their vaunted relationships.

Herrnstein and Murray's correlation coefficients are generally low enough by themselves to inspire lack of confidence. (Correlation coefficients measure the strength of linear relationships between variables; the positive values run from 0.0 for no relationship to 1.0 for perfect linear relationship.) Although low figures are not atypical for large social-science surveys involving many variables, most of Herrnstein and Murray's correlations are very weak—often in the 0.2 to 0.4 range. Now, 0.4 may sound respectably strong, but—and this is the key point—R^2 is the square of the correlation coefficient, and the square of a number between zero and one is less than the number itself, so a 0.4 correlation yields an R-squared of only .16. In Appendix 4, then, one discovers that the vast majority of the conventional measures of R^2, excluded from the main body of the text, are less than 0.1.

These very low values of R^2 expose the true weakness, in any meaningful vernacular sense, of nearly all the relationships that form the meat of *The Bell Curve*.

Like so many conservative ideologues who rail against the largely bogus ogre of suffocating political correctness, Herrnstein and Murray claim that they only want a hearing for unpopular views so that truth will out. And here, for once, I agree entirely. As a card-carrying First Amendment (near) absolutist, I applaud the publication of unpopular views that some people consider dangerous. I am delighted that *The Bell Curve* was written—so that its errors could be exposed, for Herrnstein and Murray are right to point out the difference between public and private agendas on race, and we must struggle to make an impact on the private agendas as well. But *The Bell Curve* is scarcely an academic treatise in social theory and population genetics. It is a manifesto of conservative ideology; the book's inadequate and biased treatment of data displays its primary purpose—advocacy. The text evokes the dreary and scary drumbeat of claims associated with conservative think tanks: reduction or elimination of welfare, ending or sharply curtailing affirmative action in schools and workplaces, cutting back Head Start and other forms of preschool education, trimming programs for the slowest learners and applying those funds to the gifted. (I would love to see more attention paid to talented students, but not at this cruel price.)

The penultimate chapter presents an apocalyptic vision of a society with a growing underclass permanently mired in the inevitable sloth of their low IQs. They will take over our city centers, keep having illegitimate babies (for many are too stupid to practice birth control), and ultimately require a kind of custodial state, more to keep them in check—and out of high IQ neighborhoods—than to realize any hope of amelioration, which low IQ makes impossible in any case. Herrnstein and Murray actually write, "In short, by custodial state, we have in mind a high-tech and more lavish version of the Indian reservation for some substantial minority of the nation's population, while the rest of America tries to go about its business."

The final chapter tries to suggest an alternative, but I have never read anything more grotesquely inadequate. Herrnstein and Murray yearn romantically for the good old days of towns and neighborhoods where all people could be given tasks of value, and self-esteem could be found for people on all steps of the IQ hierarchy (so Forrest Gump might collect clothing for the church raffle, while Mr. Murray and the other bright ones do the planning and keep the accounts—they have forgotten about the town Jew and the dwellers on the other side of the tracks in many of these idyllic villages). I do believe in this concept of neighborhood, and I will fight for its return. I grew up in such a place in Queens. But can anyone seriously find solutions for (rather that important palliatives of) our social ills therein?

However, if Herrnstein and Murray are wrong, and IQ represents not an immutable thing in the head, grading human beings on a single scale of general capacity with large numbers of custodial incompetents at the bottom, then the model that generates their gloomy vision collapses, and the wonderful variousness of human abilities, properly nurtured, reemerges. We must fight the doctrine of *The Bell Curve* both because it is wrong and because it will, if activated, cut off all possibility of proper nurturance for everyone's intelligence. Of course, we cannot all be rocket scientists or brain surgeons, but those who can't might be rock musicians or professional athletes (and gain far more social prestige and salary thereby), while others will indeed serve by standing and waiting.

I closed my chapter in *The Mismeasure of Man* on the unreality of *g* and the fallacy of regarding intelligence as a single-scaled, innate thing in the head with a marvelous quotation from John Stuart Mill, well worth repeating:

> The tendency has always been strong to believe that whatever received a name must be an entity or being, having an independent existence of its own, and if no real entity answering to the name could be found, men did not for that reason suppose that none existed, but imagined that it was something particularly abstruse and mysterious.

How strange that we would let a single and false number divide us, when evolution has united all people in the recency of our common ancestry—thus undergirding with a shared humanity that infinite variety which custom can never stale. *E pluribus unum.*

Cracking Open the IQ Box

HOWARD GARDNER

Despite its largely technical nature, *The Bell Curve* has already secured a prominent place in American Consciousness as a "big," "important," and "controversial" book. In a manner more befitting a chronicle of sex or spying, the publisher withheld it from potential critics until the date of publication. Since then it has grabbed front-page attention in influential publications, ridden the talk-show waves, and catalyzed academic conferences and dinner table controversies. With the untimely death of the senior author, psychologist Richard Herrnstein, attention has focused on his collaborator Charles Murray (described by the *New York Times Magazine* as the "most dangerous conservative in America"). But this volume clearly bears the mark of both men.

The Bell Curve is a strange work. Some of the analysis and a good deal of the tone are reasonable. Yet, the science in the book was questionable when it was proposed a century ago, and it has now been completely supplanted by the development of the cognitive sciences and neurosciences. The policy recommendations of the book are also exotic, neither following from the analyses nor justified on their own terms. The book relies heavily on innuendo, some of it quite frightening in its implications. The authors wrap themselves in a mantle of courage, while coyly disavowing the extreme conclusions that their own arguments invite. The tremendous attention lavished on the book probably comes less from the science or the policy proposals than from the subliminal messages and attitudes it conveys.

Taken at face value, *The Bell Curve* proceeds in straightforward

23

fashion. Herrnstein and Murray summarize decades of work in psy-chometrics and policy studies and report the results of their own extensive analyses of the National Longitudinal Survey of Labor Market Experience of Youth, a survey that began in 1979 and has followed more than 12,000 Americans aged 14–22. They argue that studies of trends in American society have steadfastly ignored a smoking gun: the increasing influence of measured intelligence (IQ). As they see it, individuals have always differed in intelligence, at least partly because of heredity, but these differences have come to matter more because social status now depends more on individ-ual achievement. The consequence of this trend is the bipolarization of the population, with high-IQ types achieving positions of power and prestige, low-IQ types being consigned to the ranks of the impoverished and the impotent. In the authors' view, the combined ranks of the poor, the criminal, the unemployed, the illegitimate (parents and offspring), and the uncivil harbor a preponderance of unintelligent individuals. Herrnstein and Murray are disturbed by these trends, particularly by the apparently increasing number of people who have babies but fail to become productive citizens. The authors foresee the emergence of a brutal society in which "the rich and the smart" (who are increasingly the same folks) band together to isolate and perhaps even reduce the ranks of those who besmirch the social fabric.

Scientifically, this is a curious work. If science is narrowly con-ceived as simply carrying out correlations and regression equations, the science in *The Bell Curve* seems, at least on a first reading, unexceptional. (My eyebrows were raised, though, by the authors' decision to introduce a new scoring system after they had com-pleted an entire draft of the manuscript. They do not spell out the reasons for this switch, nor do they indicate whether the results were different using the earlier system.) But science goes far beyond the number-crunching stereotype; scientific inquiry involves the conceptualization of problems, decisions about the kinds of data to secure and analyze, the consideration of alternative explanations, and, above all, the chain of reasoning from assumptions to findings to inferences. In this sense, the science in *The Bell Curve* is more like special pleading, based on a biased reading of the data, than a carefully balanced assessment of current knowledge.

Moreover, there is never a direct road from research to policy. One could look at the evidence presented by Herrnstein and Murray, as many of a liberal persuasion have done, and recommend targeted policies of intervention to help the dispossessed. Herrnstein and Murray, of course, proceed in quite the opposite direction. They report that efforts to raise intelligence have been unsuccessful and they oppose, on both moral and pragmatic grounds, programs of affirmative action or other ameliorative measures at school or in the workplace. Their ultimate solution, such as it is, is the restriction of a world they attribute to the Founding Fathers. These wise men acknowledged large differences in human abilities and did not try artificially to bring about equality of results; instead, Herrnstein and Murray tell us, they promoted a society in which each individual had his or her place in a local neighborhood and was accordingly valued as a human being with dignity.

The Bell Curve is well argued and admirably clear in its exposition. The authors are, for the most part, fair and thorough in laying out alternative arguments and interpretations. Presenting views that set a new standard for political incorrectness, they do so in a way that suggests their own overt discomfort—real or professed. Rush Limbaugh and Jesse Helms might like the implications, but they would hardly emulate the hedges and the "more in sorrow" statements. At least some of the authors' observations make sense. For example, their critique of the complex and often contradictory messages embodied in certain government social policies is excellent, and their recommendations for simpler rules are appropriate.

Yet I became increasingly disturbed as I read and reread this 800-page work. I gradually realized I was encountering a style of thought previously unknown to me: scholarly brinkmanship. Whether concerning an issue of science, policy, or rhetoric, the authors come dangerously close to embracing the most extreme positions, yet in the end shy away from doing so. Discussing scientific work on intelligence, they never quite say that intelligence is all-important and tied to one's genes; yet they signal that this is their belief and that readers ought to embrace the same conclusions. Discussing policy, they never quite say that affirmative action should be totally abandoned or that childbearing or immigration by those of low IQ should be curbed; yet they signal their sympathy for these options and intimate that readers ought to consider these possibilities. Finally, the rhetoric of the book encourages readers to identify with the IQ elite and to distance themselves from the dispossessed in what amounts to an invitation to class warfare. Scholarly brinkmanship encourages the reader to draw the strongest conclusions, while allowing the authors to disavow this intention.

DO GENES EXPLAIN SOCIAL CLASS?

In a textbook published in 1975, Herrnstein and his colleague Roger Brown argued that the measurement of intelligence has been the greatest achievement of twentieth-century scientific psychology. Psychometricians can make a numerical estimate of a person's intelligence that remains surprisingly stable after the age of five or so, and much convergent evidence suggests that the variations of this measure of intelligence in a population are determined significantly (at least 60 percent) by inheritable factors. As Herrnstein and Murray demonstrate at great length, measured intelligence correlates with success in school, ultimate job status, and the likelihood of becoming a member of the cognitively entitled establishment.

But correlation is not causation, and it is possible that staying in school causes IQ to go up (rather than vice versa) or that both IQ and schooling reflect some third causative factor, such as parental attention, nutrition, social class, or motivation. Indeed, nearly every one of Herrnstein and Murray's reported correlations can be challenged on such grounds. Yet, Herrnstein and Murray make a persuasive cast that measured intelligence—or, more technically, g, the central, general component of measured intelligence—does affect one's ultimate niche in society.

But the links between genetic inheritance and IQ, and then between IQ and social class, are much too weak to draw the inference that genes determine an individual's ultimate status in society. Nearly all of the reported correlations between measured intelligence and societal outcomes explain at most 20 percent of the variance. In other words, over 80 percent (and perhaps over 90 percent) of the factors contributing to socioeconomic status lie beyond measured intelligence. One's ultimate niche in society is overwhelmingly determined by non-IQ factors, ranging from initial social class to luck. And since close to half of one's IQ is due to factors unrelated to heredity, well over 90 percent of one's fate does not lie in one's genes. Inherited IQ is at most a paper airplane, not a smoking gun.

Indeed, even a sizable portion of the data reported or alluded to in *The Bell Curve* runs directly counter to the story that the authors apparently wish to tell. They note that IQ has gone up consistently around the world during this century—15 points, as great as the current difference between blacks and whites. Certainly this spurt cannot be explained by genes! They note that when blacks move from rural southern to urban northern areas, their intelligence scores also rise; that black youngsters adopted in households of higher socioeconomic status demonstrate improved performance on aptitude and achievement tests; and that differences between the performances of black and white students have declined on tests ranging from the Scholastic Aptitude Test to the National Assessment of Educational Practice. In an extremely telling phrase, Herrnstein and Murray say that the kind of direct verbal interaction between white middle-class parents and their preschool children "amounts to excellent training for intelligence tests." On that basis, they might very well have argued for expanding Head Start, but instead they question the potential value of any effort to change what they regard as the immutable power of inherited IQ.

PSYCHOLOGY, BIOLOGY, AND CULTURE

The psychometric faith in IQ testing and Herrnstein and Murray's analysis are based on assumptions that emerged a century ago, when Alfred Binet devised the first test of intelligence for children. Since 1900, biology, psychology, and anthropology have enormously advanced our understanding of the mind. But like biologists who ignore DNA or physicists who do not consider quantum mechanical effects, Herrnstein and Murray pay virtually no attention to these insights and, as a result, there is a decidedly anachronistic flavor to their entire discussion.

Intoxication with the IQ test is a professional hazard among psychometricians. I have known many psychometricians who feel that
the science of testing will ultimately lay bare all the secrets of the
mind. Some believe a difference of even a few points in an IQ or
SAT score discloses something important about an individual's or
group's intellectual merits. The world of intelligence testers is peculiarly self-contained. Like the chess player who thinks all games (if
not the world itself) are like chess, or the car salesman who speaks
only of horsepower, the psychometrician may come to believe that
all of importance in the mind can be captured by a small number of
items in the Stanford-Binet test or by one's ability to react quickly
and accurately to a pattern of lights displayed on a computer
screen.

Though Herrnstein deviated sharply in many particulars from
his mentor B. F. Skinner, the analysis in *The Bell Curve* is Skinner-
ian in a fundamental sense: It is a "black box analysis." Along with
most psychometricians, Herrnstein and Murray convey the impression that one's intelligence simply exists as an innate fact of life—
unanalyzed and unanalyzable—as if it were hidden in a black box.
Inside the box there is a single number, IQ, which determines vast
social consequences.

Outside the closed world of psychometricians, however, a more
empirically sensitive and scientifically compelling understanding of
human intelligence has emerged in the past hundred years. Many
authorities have challenged the notion of a single intelligence or
even the concept of intelligence altogether. Let me mention just a
few examples. (The works by Stephen Ceci and Robert Sternberg,
as well as my own, discuss many more.)

Sternberg and his colleagues have studied valued kinds of intel-
lect not measured by IQ tests, such as practical intelligence—the
kinds of skills and capacities valued in the workplace. They have
shown that effective managers are able to pick up various tacit messages at the workplace and that this crucial practical sensitivity is
largely unrelated to psychometric intelligence. Ralph Rosnow and
his colleagues have developed measures of social or personal intelligence—the capacities to figure out how to operate in complex

human situations—and have again demonstrated that these are unrelated to the linguistic and logical skills tapped in IQ tests.

Important new work has been carried out on the role of training in the attainment of expertise. Anders Ericsson and his colleagues have demonstrated that training, not inborn talent, accounts for much of experts' performances; the ultimate achievement of chess players or musicians depends (as your mother told you) on regular practice over many years. Ceci and others have documented the extremely high degree of expertise that can be achieved by randomly chosen individuals; for example, despite low measured intelligence, handicappers at the racetrack successfully employ astonishingly complex multiplicative models. A growing number of researchers have argued that, while IQ tests may provide a reasonable measure of certain linguistic and mathematical forms of thinking, other equally important kinds of intelligence, such as spatial, musical, or personal, are ignored (this is the subject of much of my own work). In short, the closed world of intelligence is being opened up.

Accompanying this rethinking of the concept of intelligence(s), there is growing skepticism that short paper-and-pencil tests can get at important mental capacities. Just as "performance examinations" are coming to replace multiple-choice tests in schools, many scientists, among them Lauren Resnick and Jean Lave, have probed the capacities of individuals to solve problems "on the scene" rather than in a testing room, with pencil and paper. Such studies regularly confirm that one can perform at an expert level in a natural or simulated setting (such as bargaining in a market or simulating the role of a city manager) even with a low IQ, while a high IQ cannot in itself substitute for training, expertise, motivation, and creativity. Rather than the pointless exercise of attempting to raise psychometric IQ (on which Herrnstein and Murray perseverate), this research challenges us to try to promote the actual behavior and skills that we want our future citizens to have. After all, if we found that better athletes happen to have larger shoe sizes, we would hardly try to enlarge the feet of the less athletic.

Scientific understanding of biological and cultural aspects of cognition also grows astonishingly with every passing decade. Virtually no serious natural scientist speaks about genes and environment any longer as if they were opposed. Indeed, every serious investigator accepts the importance of both biological and cultural factors and the need to understand their interactions. Genes regulate all human behavior, but no form of behavior will emerge without the appropriate environment triggers or supports. Learning alters the way in which genes are expressed.

The development of the individual brain and mind begins in utero, and pivotal alterations in capacity and behavior come about as the result of innumerable events following conception. Hormonal effects in utero, which certainly are environmental, can cause a different profile of cognitive strengths and limitations to emerge. The loss of certain sensory capacities causes the redeployment of brain tissue to new functions; a rich environment engenders the growth of additional cortical connections as well as timely pruning of excess synapses. Compare a child who has a dozen healthy experiences each day in utero and after birth to another child who has a daily diet of a dozen injurious episodes. The cumulative advantage of healthy prenatal environment and a stimulating postnatal environment is enormous. In the study of IQ, much has been made of studies of identical and fraternal twins. But because of the influences on cognition in utero and during infancy, even such studies cannot decisively distinguished genetic from environmental influences.

Herrnstein and Murray note that measured intelligence is only stable after age five, without drawing the obvious conclusion that the events of the first years of life, not some phlogiston-like g, are the principal culprit. Scores of important and fascinating new findings emerge in neuroscience every year, but scarcely a word of any of this penetrates the Herrnstein and Murray black-box approach.

Precisely the same kind of story can be told from the cultural perspective. Cultural beliefs and practices affect the child at least from the moment of birth and perhaps sooner. Even the parents' expectations of their unborn child and their reactions to the discovery of the child's sex have an impact. The family, teachers, and other sources of influence in the culture signal what is important to the growing child, and these messages have both short- and long-term impact. How one thinks about oneself, one's prospects in this world and beyond, and whether one regards intelligence as inborn or acquired—all these shape patterns of activity, attention, and personal investments in learning and self-improvement. Particularly for stigmatized minorities, these signals can wreck any potential for cognitive growth and achievement.

Consider Claude Steele's research on the effects of stereotyping on performance. African-American students perform worse than white students when they are led to believe that the test is an intellectual one and that their race matters, but these differences wash out completely when such "stereotype vulnerable" conditions are removed.

To understand the effects of culture, no study is more seminal than Harold Stevenson and James Stigler's book *The Learning Gap: Why Our Schools Are Failing and What We Can Learn from Japanese and Chinese Education* (1992). In an analysis that runs completely counter to *The Bell Curve*, Stevenson and Stigler show why Chinese and Japanese students achieve so much more in schools than do Americans. They begin by demonstrating that initial differences in IQ among the three populations are either nonexistent or trivial. But with each passing year, East Asian students raise their edge over Americans, so that by the middle school years, there is virtually no overlap in reading and mathematics performance between the two populations.

Genetics, heredity, and measured intelligence play no role here. East Asian students learn more and score better on just about every kind of measure because they attend school for more days, work harder in school and at home after school, and have better-prepared teachers and more deeply engaged parents who encourage and coach them each day and night. Put succinctly, Americans believe (like Herrnstein and Murray) that if you do not do well, it is because they lack talent or ability; Asians believe it is because they do not work hard enough. As a Japanese aphorism has it, "Fail with five hours of sleep; pass with four." Both predictions tend to be self-fulfilling. As educator Derek Bok once quipped, Americans score near to last on almost all measures save one: When you ask Americans how they *think* they are doing, they profess more satisfaction than any other group. Like Herrnstein and Murray, most Americans have not understood that what distinguishes the cultures is the pattern of self-understanding and motivation, especially the demands that we make on ourselves (and on those we care about) and the lessons we draw from success and failure—not the structure of genes or the shape of the brain.

THE SHAKY BRIDGE TO POLICY

Like Murray's earlier book *Losing Ground, The Bell Curve* views most recent governmental attempts at intervention doing more harm than good and questions the value of welfare payments, affirmative action programs, indeed, and kind of charitable disposition toward the poor. To improve education, Herrnstein and Murray recommended vouchers to encourage a private market and put forth the remarkable proposal that the government should shift funds from disadvantaged to gifted children. And while they do not openly endorse policies that will limit breeding among the poor or keep the dispossessed from our shores, they stimulate us to consider such possibilities.

Nowhere did I find the Herrnstein and Murray analysis less convincing than in their treatment of crime. Incarcerated offenders, they point out, have an average IQ of 92, eight points below the national mean. They go on to suggest that since lower cognitive aptitude is associated with higher criminal activity, there would be less crime if IQs were higher. But if intelligence levels have at worst been constant, why did crime increase so much between the 1960s and the 1980s? Why have crime rates leveled off and declined in the last few years? Does low IQ also explain the embarrassing prevalence of white-collar crime in business and politics or the recent sudden rise in crime in Russia? Astonishingly, no other influences, such as the values promoted by the mass media, play any role in Herrnstein and Murray's analysis.

Considering how often they remind us that the poor and benighted at society's bottom are incapable through no fault of their own, Herrnstein and Murray's hostility to efforts to reduce poverty might seem, at the very least, ungenerous. But, at the book's end, the authors suddenly turn from their supposed unblinking realism to fanciful nostalgia. Having consigned the dispossessed to a world where they can achieve little because of their own meager intellectual gifts, Herrnstein and Murray call on the society as a whole to reconstitute itself: to become (once again?) a world of neighborhoods where each individual is made to feel important, valued, and dignified. They devote not a word to how this return to lost neighborhoods is to be brought about or how those with low IQs and no resources could suddenly come to feel worthwhile. It is as if we were watching scenes from *Apocalypse Now* or *Natural Born Killers,* only to blink for a minute and to find the movie concluding with images from a situation comedy or "Mr. Roger's Neighborhood."

RHETORICAL BOMB-THROWING

Perhaps the most troubling aspect of the book is its rhetorical stance. This is one of the most stylistically divisive books that I have ever read. Despite occasional avowals of regret and the few utopian pages at the end, Herrnstein and Murray set up an us-them dichotomy that eventually culminates in an us-*against*-them opposition.

Who are "we"? Well, we are the people who went to Harvard (as the jacket credits both of the authors) or attended similar colleges and read books like this. We are the smart, the rich, the powerful, the worriers. And who are "they"? They are the pathetic others, those who could not get into good schools and who don't cut it on IQ tests and SATs. While perhaps perfectly nice people, they are simply not going to make it in tomorrow's complex society and will probably end up cordoned off from the rest of us under the tutelage of a vicious custodial state. The hope for a civil society depends on a miraculous return of the spirit of the Founding Fathers to re-create the villages of Thomas Jefferson or George Bailey (as played by Jimmy Stewart) or Beaver Cleaver (as played by Jerry Mather).

How is this rhetorical polarization achieved? At literally dozens of points in the book, Herrnstein and Murray seek to stress the extent to which they and the readers resemble one another and differ from those unfortunate souls who cause our society's problems.

Reviewing *The Bell Curve* of the title, Herrnstein and Murray declare, in a representative passage:

> You—meaning the self-selected person who has read this far into this book—live in a world that probably looks nothing like the figure. In all likelihood, almost all of your friends and professional associates belong to that top Class I slice. Your friends and associates who you consider to be unusually slow are probably somewhere in Class II.

Why is this so singularly off-putting? I would have thought it unnecessary to say, but if people as psychometrically smart as Messrs. Herrnstein and Murray did not "get it," it is safer to be explicit. High IQ doesn't make a person one whit better than anybody else. And if we are to have any chance of a civil and humane society, we had better avoid the smug self-satisfaction of an elite that reeks of arrogance and condescension.

Though there are seven appendices, spanning over 100 pages, and nearly 200 pages of footnotes, bibliography, and index, one element is notably missing from this tome: a report on any program of social intervention that works. For example, Herrnstein and Murray never mention Lisbeth Schorr's *Within Our Reach: Breaking the Cycle of Disadvantage*, a book that was prompted in part by *Losing Ground*. Schorr chronicles a number of social programs that have made a genuine difference in education, child health service, family planning, and other lightning-rod areas of our society. And to the ranks of the programs chronicled in Schorr's book, many new names can now be added. Those who have launched Interfaith Educational Agencies, City Year, Teach for America, Jobs for the Future, and hundreds of other service agencies have not succumbed to the sense of futility and abandonment of the poor that the Herrnstein and Murray book promotes.

When I recently debated Murray on National Public Radio, he was reluctant to accept the possibility that programs of intervention might dissolve or significantly reduce differences in intelligence. If he did, the entire psychometric edifice that he and Herrnstein have constructed would collapse. While claiming to confront facts that others refuse to see, they are blind to both contradictory evidence and the human consequences of their work. Herrnstein and Murray, of course, have the right to their conclusions. But if they truly believe that blacks will not be deeply hurt by the hints that they are genetically inferior, they are even more benighted—dare I say, even more stupid—than I have suggested.

It is callous to write a work that casts earlier attempts to help the disadvantaged in the least-favorable light, strongly suggests that nothing positive can be done in the present climate, contributes to an us-against-them mentality, and then posits a miraculous cure. High intelligence and high creativity are desirable. But unless they are linked to some kind of moral compass, their possessors might best be consigned to an island of glass-bead game players, with no access to the mainland.

Race, IQ, and Scientism

RICHARD NISBETT

The Bell Curve has all the trappings of a scientific work, including great length, endless statistics, and an enormous number of references. Partly because of these attributes, both scientists and laypeople tend to make some tacit assumptions about the book: that important evidence relevant to a point will be presented, that it will be accurately described, and that it will be interpreted in line with the normal canons of science.

Readers making such assumptions about *The Bell Curve* would be obliged to feel that there is very strong support for three propositions: 1) The races differ genetically in such a way as to account for a substantial portion of the fifteen point (one standard deviation) difference in IQ between blacks and whites. 2) Interventions designed to improve cognitive skills have very small and ephemeral effects. 3) Partly as a consequence of (1) and (2), there has been little if any convergence in IQ between blacks and whites in recent decades despite a reduction in racism and improved educational and economic opportunity for blacks.

In fact, however, *The Bell Curve* presents nothing like the full range of relevant evidence concerning either the question of genetic differences between the races in intelligence (the B/W gap in the terminology of *The Bell Curve*) or the question of intervention; and, though the book's coverage of the question of the evidence concerning convergence is copious, their summary of that evidence is factually wrong and the speculations about convergence are at variance with the facts and common sense.

GENETICS, RACE, AND IQ

RACIAL ANCESTRY

There are seven studies that have found their way into the general literature on race and IQ that allow us to assess in a direct way the effects of genetics on IQ. These are studies that attempt to reduce or eliminate the real-world confounding of race with environment—that is, the fact that blacks and whites live in different environments with different forms of socialization and different opportunities. Some studies compare blacks and whites raised in the same environment. Other studies take advantage of the fact that the "black" population includes many individuals with partially, or even primarily European ancestry. If European ancestry for "blacks" is associated with higher IQs, this suggests a genetic contribution to the IQ gap. All such studies suffer from inherent flaws, but at least the flaws are different for different studies, a situation which in principle could allow for relatively strong inferences.

Except for a one-paragraph dismissal of one of the studies in the text and dismissal of a second in a footnote at the end of the book, *The Bell Curve* reports on only one of the European heritage studies: an adoption study by Sandra Scarr and Richard Weinberg[1] in which white parents raised adopted children of different racial backgrounds. Some of the adopted children had two white parents, some had two black parents, and some had one black and one white parent. The white adoptees had higher IQs than the mixed-race adoptees, who in turn had higher IQs than the black adoptees. Herrnstein and Murray hold that the results strongly indicated a partial genetic contribution to the B/W gap. Scarr and Weinberg themselves, however, believe that the data are simply not informative about whether the B/W gap they found was due to racial genetic differences or to social racial discrimination.

Herrnstein and Murray do not mention any of the problems with the study that critics (including Scarr and Weinberg themselves) have identified: the number of children involved was small (only 25 white children and 29 black children); there could have been selec tive placement by the adoption agencies; the adoptive families were recruited on a voluntary basis, which could have introduced a "self-selection" problem into the sample; the natural parents' IQs were not known, allowing for the possibility that the white parents could have had higher (genotypic) IQs than the black parents, which by itself would lead to the expectation that the white adoptees would be expected to have higher IQs than the black adoptees; and the black children were adopted at a substantially later age than the white children (though the mixed-race children were adopted earlier than any). Perhaps most importantly, the family was only one source of influence on development and IQ was surely affected by factors outside the home including quite possibly adjustment problems caused by being a black member of a white family.[2]

The authors do not mention another comparable study in which black and white children in a residential institution were compared.[3] The study has many of the same problems as the Scarr-Weinberg study, most importantly that the IQs of the natural parents were not known. But the study had the advantage that the children were all raised in the same enriched institutional environment, thus there was no question of self-selection or differential placement. At four or five years of age, the white children had IQs of 103, the black children had IQs of 108, and the children of mixed race had IQs of 106. On the face of it, these results are most compatible with the assumption of a slight genetic superiority for blacks. The blacks in question were West Indian and the white children English. It is of course possible that the black parents had very unusually high IQs, but selective migration of West Indians to Britain is not likely to have been a factor.[4]

The only racial ancestry study other than that by Scarr and Weinberg that the authors deal with in the text is one in which several hundred German children fathered by black GIs in World War II were compared to those fathered by white GIs. The children fathered by black GIs had an average IQ of 96.5 and the children fathered by white GIs had an average IQ of 97. For this study, the authors are worried about self-selection: "The actual IQs of the fathers were unknown, and therefore a variety of selection factors cannot be ruled out" (p. 310). While true, the simplest account is to assume approximately equal (genotypic) IQs of black and white fathers inasmuch as the (phenotypic) B/W gap in the military as a whole was probably close to that in the general population and the degree of self-selection on the basis of IQ would have had to be implausibly great in order to produce the results obtained.[5] (If indeed any self-selection on the basis of IQ would be expected for unions that would not result in marriage for either the blacks or the whites.) The psychologist James Flynn has argued that the model that best fits the data is one that assumes zero heritability of the B/W gap in the U.S. population as a whole.[6]

Two other studies take a quite different approach to the question of racial ancestry. These studies took advantage of two facts: 1) the "black" population in the United States consists of from 20–30 percent European genes and 2) Africans and Europeans differ in blood group genes sufficiently to be able to obtain a measure of the degree of "Europeanness" of an individual's heritage. Under the genetic hypothesis, the more the European genes, the higher the IQ should be. In fact, however, the correlation between estimated European heritage and IQ for a sample of 288 young blacks in Philadelphia was a trivial and nonsignificant .05.[7] The authors mention the study only in a note at the end of the book, and mention it there only to dismiss it on the grounds of self-selection: one does not know about the intelligence of the white ancestors and the study is thus not very probative because, if the white ancestors were particularly unintelligent, it might be no advantage for a black to have European genes. But of course, there is no reason to assume that white ancestors who entered into unions were particularly unintelligent, and once again, the nature of the self-selection would have to have been extreme to produce the results.

The authors do not mention at all another study examining the correlation between European blood groups and IQ.[8] This study correlated the estimated Europeanness of the blood groups (rather than the estimated Europeanness of individuals based on the blood groups) with IQ in two different small samples of blacks. In one sample, the correlation was a trivial .01; in the other a nonsignificant -.38, with the more African blood groups being associated with the higher IQs.*

Another important study took yet a different approach to the question of white ancestry.[9] Imagine that the B/W difference of fifteen IQ points is fully genetic, and think of two different groups of blacks: one consisting of those having only African genes and one having 30 percent European genes. On the pure genetic model, the first group would be expected to have an IQ four or five points lower than the second. A person chosen randomly from the first group would be only somewhat likely to have an IQ higher than a person chosen randomly from the second group. But if we were to single out everyone from either group who had an extremely high IQ—say of 140, matters would be very different. We would expect to find very few such people in either group, of course, but because of the shape of *The Bell Curve*, which exaggerates population differences at the tails, we would find several times as many individuals in the high European-gene group as in the pure-African gene group. Do we?

The study identified 63 children in a sample of black Chicago schoolchildren with IQs of 125 or above and 28 with IQs of 140 or above. On the basis of their self reports about ancestry, the investigators classified the children into several categories of Europeanness. The children with IQs of 125 or above, as well as those with IQs of 140 or above, were slightly less likely to have substantial European ancestry than was estimated to be characteristic of the U.S. black population as a whole at the time. The study is not ideal—one would have preferred for the degree of European ancestry of high IQ children to be compared to the black schoolchildren of Chicago rather than to the U.S. population as a whole, and like all others, the study suffers from the possibility of self-selection. But once again, on the face of it, the results are most consistent with a model of zero genetic contribution to the B/W gap.

There is a final racial ancestry study that uses a methodology

---

*The blood group studies are not quite as persuasive as they seem, however, for technical reasons related to the fact that white blood genes are only very weakly if at all associated with one another in the black population. If not, then they might also not be associated with the white genes associated with high IQ.

completely different from those above. Under the assumption that mothers are more important than fathers to the intellectual socialization of their children and that socialization practices of whites favor the adoption of skills that result in high scores on IQ tests, one would expect that the children of unions where the mother is white and the father is black would have higher IQs than the children of unions where the mother is black and the father is white. And in fact, this is the case.[10] Children of black-white unions have IQs nine points higher if it is the mother who is white. Once again, we have a self-selection possibility, which in fact the investigators were able to assess. White fathers were further below the white male mean in school grades completed than the comparable population of white males, which would indicate lower IQ for them and hence lower genetic value than for the unions where it is the black who was the father. However, half of the white mothers were unwed, which is an even stronger indication of low IQ, since at the time of the study (1974), only about 10 percent of white mothers were unwed and these were very disproportionately of lower socioeconomic status. Thus, under any reasonable assumptions about the correlation between school grade attainment and IQ, the higher IQs of the children born to white mothers would have to be attributed largely to socialization.[11]

So what do we have? There are a total of seven studies providing direct evidence on the question of a genetic basis for the B/W IQ gap. Six of them are consistent with a zero genetic contribution to the gap (or with very slight African superiority) based just on the raw IQ numbers, and though all of these six suffer from some interpretive difficulties, they mostly boil down to a single objection. If it was very low IQ whites who mated with blacks (or very high IQ blacks who mated with whites), the results could be explained away. (One study, which compared blacks and whites in the same institutional environment, is free from this objection.) The self-selection factor would have had to be implausibly great, however, and would have had to be present under a variety of circumstances, in several very different locales, at several different time periods. The remaining study—the only one that the authors write about at any length—is at least on the face of it consistent with a model assuming a substantial genetic contribution to the B/W gap. But that study has as many interpretive problems as the others, including the two studies which the authors mention only to dismiss. Any reader would surely reach very different conclusions about the likely degree of genetic contribution to the B/W gap by virtue of knowing the facts just presented than by reading the highly selective review presented in *The Bell Curve*.

THE ARGUMENTS FOR GENETIC DETERMINATION OF THE B/W DIFFERENCE IN IQ

There are many indirect tests of the genetic hypothesis—some favoring and some opposing—which have been the basis for discussion for decades, but the indirect findings that Herrnstein and Murray seem to regard as central, given that they devote many pages to them, are the following three.

1. Blacks at every level of socioeconomic status have IQs that are lower than those of whites of the same socioeconomic status, hence it is difficult to argue that is only poor socioeconomic conditions that produce low IQs for blacks.

2. There are differences in the ability profiles of blacks and whites. Whites of low socioeconomic status having a given overall IQ score, say of 105, show the same ability pattern on average as whites of high socioeconomic status having the same overall IQ score. But this is not the case for blacks, whose ability patterns at the same given score of 105 are different from those of whites of either high or low socioeconomic status. For example, blacks at the same IQ level as whites are likely to have relatively high ability to recall digit strings but relatively low ability to solve mazes, as compared to whites.

3. Jensen and others have shown that it is on the most "*g*-loaded" tasks that blacks and whites differ most. *G* is jargon for the general intelligence factor that some psychologists believe permeates all abilities, but some more than others. For simple memory or reaction time tasks, blacks do as well or better than whites; whereas for more complex memory or reaction-time tasks having higher *g*-loadings, they are slower.

Let us consider each of these points in turn.

1. *Blacks have lower IQs at every socioeconomic level.* On the face of it, this finding is hard to reconcile with the notion that it is merely poor opportunity that causes low IQ in blacks. The first thing to note about this finding, however, is that it is quite misleading to compare, as the authors do, the IQs of blacks in the higher socioeconomic ranges with those of whites. A white in the top socioeconomic quintile based on income has more than twice the wealth of a black in the top quintile.[12] A still more important point is to note what happens when one adds to the socioeconomic measurement of opportunity several measures of the environment that include family and neighborhood structural and resource measures including measures of the learning environment. When this adjustment is made, the blacks at a given "opportunity level" are now very close to the whites at a given level.[13] Herrnstein and Murray note correctly that such attempts to equate for the full range of environmental variables are based on purely correlational data: it could in principle be the case that mother's IQ drives the other variables. However, the same regression equation that produces the results just presented predicts nothing more when mother's IQ is included. The data are thus more consistent with a purely environmental interpretation of the B/W gap than with one that leans on a genetic interpretation.

2. *Differences in the ability profiles of blacks and whites.* Such differences hardly seem a strong argument for genetic determination of overall IQ. There are systematic differences in the socialization of black and white children that begin in the cradle. It would scarcely be surprising if these affected ability patterns. And we know that purely social factors can affect ability patterns. Over the last couple of decades, while men's and women's verbal SAT scores have remained close (with men actually moving up a bit in the direction of women), women have removed half the difference in math performance that used to separate them from men. It is not unreasonable to suggest that this shift in women's math performance is a response to changes in perceived occupational opportunities. An

elegant illustration of this point comes from a natural experiment produced by World War II. Fathers were absent at different points in their children's lives for differing periods of time. For male Harvard students whose fathers had been in the Army for a long time when they were quite young, Scholastic Aptitude Test (SAT) scores were dramatically shifted away from the typical male pattern in the direction of relatively high verbal scores.

3. *It is on "g-loaded" tests that blacks and whites differ most.* Jensen and others have argued that the finding of greater speed for whites on complex reaction-time tasks, but equal speed for on the less *g*-loaded simple reaction time tasks, could not be explained by motivational differences between blacks and white, but this will have to be established by hard labor, not accomplished by postulation. In informal work conducted many years ago I found that white college students who were high in achievement motivation had faster complex reaction times, but not faster simple reaction times, than those low in achievement motivation, so I do not regard the motivation hypothesis as being in the slightest improbable.

Jensen's "*g*-loading" point also obtains for tasks that we think of as genuinely intellectual ones. For skills such as spatial reasoning and form perception, the *g*-loading is relatively low and the B/W gap relatively low. For the even more important and general skills of reading comprehension, mathematics, vocabulary and information tests, the *g*-loading is high and the B/W gap is high.

Interestingly, it is these more important, more "*g*-loaded" skills that one would assume to be modifiable. Are they?

THE EFFECTS OF INTERVENTION
ON COGNITIVE SKILLS

The entire tenor of the book's discussion of the effects of intervention is that it is very difficult to affect IQ or cognitive skills by very much or for very long. This of course lends still greater credence to the notion that we are stuck with the big B/W gap. If intervention has no effect, or if it is a rising tide that lifts all boats, then the gap will remain.

Herrnstein and Murray are strangely selective in their reports about the effects of intervention. They discuss only two studies of intervention in infancy, in each of which the subjects were at risk for retardation. One is the so-called "Milwaukee project," in which infants were given extremely enriched environments.[14] IQ gains occurred early and were still marked in adolescence. The authors dismiss this study on the grounds that there were no gains in school performance, indicating that the experimental group had gained essentially only IQ test-coaching from the intervention. The other project the authors discuss is the Abecedarian Project of Ramey and his colleagues, in which children at risk of very low IQs were placed in extremely enriched environments.[15] Substantial IQ gains were observed almost immediately and were sustained into adolescence. School performance was also superior for the experimental group. But because the gains were present in the first year or two, Herrnstein and Murray are highly skeptical, arguing that the results could be due to a failure to assign children randomly to groups.

Perhaps the authors were unaware of the very large literature that exists on the topic of early intervention and which literally precludes the possibilities that only noncognitive, "coaching" gains occur or that nonrandom assignment could account for the results. For example, a multisite study published in *Pediatrics* in 1992 showed a nine point IQ advantage at age three as a consequence of early intervention for at-risk infants (those born prematurely or having low birth weight).[16]

Herrnstein and Murray also discuss post-infancy intervention in the preschool years. They accept the conclusions of the experts in the field that very vigorous intervention programs can produce IQ gains of around seven points by the time children enter school, but regard this as not very impressive because these gains begin to fade immediately and are largely gone several years after the programs are completed. And yet it should be obvious that, if environmental factors are important at all, as indeed is established by the very substantial effects of the intervention, then once the environment reverts to one that is non-enriched, the cognitive gains would be expected to fade. If the enrichment were to continue, perhaps the intellectual gains would too.

And indeed this is what happens, although Herrnstein and Murray do not discuss this fact at all. When preschool intervention is followed by intervention in the early school years, the intellectual gains are to a substantial extent sustained.[17] And even if the intervention is begun only during the school years, very marked improvement can still be seen. William Bennett, the former Secretary of Education, has written of the many interventions from elementary school through high school that have been shown to be effective.[18] It apparently does not require heroic efforts or huge expenditures to raise the academic performance of minority children in impoverished schools.

Herrnstein and Murray discuss one elementary school study only—Project Intelligence in Venezuela that assigned hundreds of children randomly to an experimental group that received sixty additional 45 minute lessons intended to improve reasoning, vocabulary, and other skills over the course of a year.[19] The experimental group gained a net .1 standard deviation on a "culture-fair" test and a net .4 standard deviations on a conventional IQ test. Thus a rather modest intervention yielded in a single year an IQ gain of between 1.6 and 6.5 points. The authors, perhaps because they are unaware of the educational effects closer to home, refuse to become excited about these results on the grounds that, since the project only continued for one year, it is possible that subsequent years would have produced no gain or even allowed a fade-out.

Finally, the authors discuss the coaching effects for the SAT tests, citing studies on the effects of differing amounts of study. Even though coaching is not directed to at-risk or minority populations, they do speak to the question of the skill gains that might be possible for adolescents. The gains can be treated as IQ score gains by virtue of the high correlations that SAT scores, particularly verbal scores, have with IQ test scores. The effect of coaching programs (according to a report by ETS staffers), is modest but scarcely trivial for verbal SAT, producing the equivalent of three IQ points for the investment of about fifty hours of work. The effects of coaching on the math portion are greater, resulting in a gain equivalent to about five IQ points with about sixty-five hours of work (converting math scores to IQ scores is however less justified than allowing verbal scores to represent IQ). Once again, the authors accentuate the negative. Coaching effects reach an asymptote rather soon, producing little gain after about ninety hours, so they find little to cheer about. There is actually reason to suspect, however, that the early asymptote might be limited to students who have come close to reaching their potential. When minority students are put into accelerated mathematics programs, the results can be dramatic, with levels of achievement exceeding that of other minority students by enormous margins.[20]

The authors do not deal at all with the effects of college interventions. Yet there are many of these around the country, some with very large documented effects on the performance of minority group members. The mathematician Urie Treisman,[21] for example, has intervened in introductory math education in college, where blacks often perform poorly not only with respect to whites but disappointingly with respect to their own entering credentials. Introductory math is crucial because it is the entry card to the sciences. Poor grades essentially disqualify a first-year student from these courses and the careers they make possible. Noting that black students often lack the intellectual networks of whites and Asians, Treisman set up rigorous coaching sessions in which blacks were encouraged to study together with other students, including whites and Asians as well as blacks, and to deal with harder problems than the course itself provided. Any hint of remediation was avoided, and in fact was not present. The results were dramatic. Most black students without the program received either D or F. Blacks who went through the program drastically improved, actually outperforming whites not in the program who had higher SAT math scores. In human—and human capital—terms, the intervention was enough to make the difference between a terminal degree and math performance good enough to keep the typical black student on track in engineering school or in good position to be attractive to medical schools. The Treisman intervention does not depend on the charisma of a single individual nor the characteristics of a particular college setting. It has been duplicated at least a dozen times around the country.

Many other interventions are also successful at the college level, for individual courses and more importantly for overall grades. It has been argued by psychologist Claude Steele[22] that a characteristic of the more successful interventions is that, though they improve the performance of whites, they improve the performance of blacks far more. Apparently there are many aspects of college life that, despite the best intentions of teachers and administrators, make things less than ideal for minority students. We are gradually learning what those aspects are and how they can be changed.

Note that all that is required to establish modifiability of cognitive skills and the feasibility of reducing the B/W IQ gap are "existence proofs." If one can show in addition that there are programs having strong effects that can be duplicated at other sites with other personnel, then the pragmatic case for intervention is fully made. And despite the selective review and relentless pessimism of Herrnstein and Murray, we have both existence proofs and multi-site demonstrations at every stage of childhood and youth. Although white middle-class youngsters have very great advantages, it is possible to improve the cognitive skills of less privileged, minority youngsters and to reduce the differences between the two groups.

CONVERGENCE IN IQ

Existence proofs of intervention success aside, is it possible to show that, after thirty years of improved educational and economic opportunity for blacks, there is in fact any reduction in the B/W gap? If not, demonstrations of the effectiveness of intervention would be the equivalent of hothouse plants. If changed conditions have not resulted in a reduction in the fifteen point gap, outside of specially created programs, we would have to wonder if convergence was ever going to be a reality, and it would cause us to reflect again on the possibility that the B/W gap is to some substantial extent genetic.

The authors' treatment of the topic of convergence is quite different from their treatment of the issues of genetic determination and intervention effects, for which they combine the leaving out of crucial evidence with a heavy-handed, negative interpretation of the data they do report. For the issue of convergence, Herrnstein and

Murray review, so far as I can tell, most of the pertinent evidence.

The evidence is of two kinds: cognitive skills tests such as reading, mathematics, and science, and actual IQ test scores. Skills tests, especially the verbal portions, correlate sufficiently highly with IQ scores to justify using them as a proxy for IQ. And of course we care at least as much whether academic skills are converging as we care whether IQ scores are converging.

To simplify the reporting of the academic skills data, I will present the average degree of convergence for the five data sources the book presents in the form of degree of improvement in composite scores (verbal or reading plus math, or reading plus math and science). The best of the data sources is the National Assessment of Educational Progress (NAEP), based on a random sample of thousands of American students of age nine, thirteen, and seventeen. The reduction in B/W gap for the composite score over a period of about twenty years ending in 1990 was equal to .28 standard deviations, or 4.2 IQ points. Another long-duration study the authors report is the change in B/W gap in SAT scores over a seventeen-year period ending in 1993. This was a reduction of almost a third of a standard deviation, equivalent to five IQ points for a two-decade period. There are also three shorter term studies lasting about a decade. The National High School Studies showed a reduction in B/W gap of about .15 standard deviations over a ten year period ending in 1982, which is equivalent to a 4.5 point reduction for a two-decade period. The B/W gap in American College Test (ACT) scores decreased by .16 standard deviations over an eleven-year period ending in 1991, which is equivalent to slightly less than a 4.4 point reduction over a two-decade period. The B/W gap in GRE scores decreased by .17 standard deviations over a nine-year period ending in 1988, which is equivalent to a 5.7 reduction over a two-decade period. Each of these results is compatible with the following generalization: the B/W gap has been decreasing by about 2.5 IQ points per decade. This would indicate that, assuming the gap was fifteen points two decades prior to around 1990, the gap in 1990 was only around ten points.

What about actual IQ scores? Here the data are even more encouraging. One review of four normative studies showed a contemporary gap of only seven IQ points for the Ravens Progressive Matrices test (a very well-known, supposedly culture-fair test). The same seven point gap was indicated by the Kaufman Assessment Battery for Children. Two normative studies employing the Stanford-Binet test (perhaps the best known of all IQ tests) indicate a contemporary gap of ten points. How should we think about these data, which on the surface would appear to be extremely optimistic? "Qualifications must be attached to these findings" (p. 290). Why? Because a critic (Arthur Jensen) warns that there may be artifacts in the sample for the K-ABC test. Suppose we yield entirely to Jensen and drop the K-ABC results. We are left with estimates of a contemporary B/W IQ gap of between seven and ten points, congruent with the estimate based on skills tests of a contemporary B/W gap of ten points.

What is the authors' summary of these data—bearing in mind that I have summarized every study they present, that the median estimate of the reduction of the B/W gap is six points, and that *not a single study indicates a narrowing of the B/W gap over the past two decades by less than 4.2 points?* Here is what the authors say on p. 292:

> Let us assume that during the past two decades black and white cognitive ability as measured by IQ has in fact converged by an amount that is consistent with the convergence in educational aptitude measures such as the SAT or NAEP—a narrowing of approximately .15 to .25 standard deviation units, or the equivalent of *two to three points overall.* (Emphasis added.) Why have the scores converged? The answer calls for speculation.

How can the authors transform the four to eight point B/W gap reduction into a two to three point reduction? Well, we are told, because in a later chapter they will present evidence showing the opposite of all the good news they have just reported. These data come from the National Longitudinal Survey of Youth (NLSY), and they are not a report of change in children's IQs at all, but a comparison at a fixed point in time of mothers' and children's IQs in a sample so unrepresentative of the U.S. population that the average IQ of the children was 92, more than one-half of a standard deviation below the mean. The authors, in an uncharacteristically opaque passage, ask us not to be troubled by this apparently aberrant sample, because the NLSY codebook tells us that "sampling weights make the results 'representative of the children of a nationally representative sample of women' who were of certain age ranges in the years the tests were given—which is subtly but importantly different from being a representative sample of American children" (p. 355).

Importantly yes, subtly no. The women in the sample were not finished with their childbearing years and the children would have been born to younger mothers who tend to come from lower socioeconomic strata. This explains why the children have IQs so much lower than the overall population mean.

The gap in the raw IQ scores separating blacks and whites is four points greater for the children than for the mothers. This is the basis for the authors' assertion that the NLSY data show that the B/W gap is increasing. What a comparison of the mother IQ gap with the child IQ gap could possibly mean is not clear given the highly unrepresentative sample (especially since, as the authors fail to point out, the B/W gap is different for the very youngest mothers in the sample than for those somewhat older).[23] But a comparison of *raw score* differences is particularly meaningless given that the sample mean for the children departs so far from the population mean. To do so is to compare the mothers' oranges with the children's apples. To adjust for this, it would be necessary to compare the B/W gap for the mothers in standard deviation form with the B/W gap for the children in standard deviation form.[24] As the authors admit (p. 356), the gap separating black and white mothers is 1.17 standard deviations *on the mothers' test* and the gap separating black and white children is 1.17 standard deviations *on the children's test*. Taken at face value, this would indicate no difference in the B/W gap for the mothers and the B/W gap for children.

But the numbers cannot be taken at face value. For a black woman to have children at a young age is not at all unusual; thus one would expect the IQ of young black mothers to be relatively close to the mean for young black women. For a white woman to have children at a very young age is more unusual—more characteristic of the low socioeconomic end of the distribution for whites than for the middle or high end—and one would expect such women to have lower IQs than the white population at large. Hence the IQs of black and white mothers should be artifactually close in the NLSY sample. But because of the regression principle, the children of white mothers would be expected to be closer to the relatively high white mean than the mothers themselves are, while the children of black mothers should be about as close as their mothers to the relatively low black mean. Since the B/W gaps in standard deviation form for mothers and children are equal when they would be expected to be greater for children on artifactual grounds having to do with regression, the data are better read as support for the view that the B/W gap is decreasing than with the view that it is increasing. (Though the number of assumptions that have to be made to wring any meaning from these data will be too great for the tastes of many social scientists.)

Having dispatched to their satisfaction with the contention that there has been any significant reduction at all in the B/W gap, the authors proceed to argue that even the tiny reduction that may have occurred to this point has stalled out, or possibly even begun to reverse itself. First, they argue, the convergence has taken place in part because the intellectual performance of whites has suffered by "slowing down to the speed of the slowest ship in the convoy" (p. 294). (This is not true. In the twenty years preceding 1990, whites improved slightly in most NAEP tests while blacks improved substantially.[25] Convergence on the SAT was similarly due to improved black performance and not worsened white performance.[26]) Second, we are asked to consider the analogy with "the increases in height that follow from better nutrition: Better nutrition helps raise the height of children whose diets would otherwise have been inadequate, but it does not add anything to the height of those who have been receiving a good diet already" (p. 295). Blacks, who "are shifted toward the lower end of the socioeconomic range," will benefit more from improvements to schooling and the greater information flow coming from the media. By continued analogy with the nutrition case, the convergence has probably now stalled out, because, although the authors do not state it in so many words, the socioeconomic leveling process has now largely run its course. The authors cite three aspects of the data in support of the speculations that the convergence has run its course. 1) The B/W gap on the NAEP has stalled. (This is true—since 1988 or 1990 the improvement has stopped or been reversed for most tests for most age groups.)[27] 2) The gap has not decreased over the past few years for the SAT. (This is technically correct but probably not reflective of the true state of affairs—the Educational Testing Service regards the gap as continuing to decrease because, although the scores of blacks and whites have remained the same, the percentage of the white population taking the tests has decreased [leaving a more selective sample of whites] while the percentage of blacks continues to increase [leaving a less selective sample of blacks],[28] and, as the authors themselves note, the convergence continues on the ACT.) 3) Most of the improvement of black SAT scores is due to decreases in the number scoring at the very bottom of the test, giving credence to the nutrition analogy. (This is not a sensible analogy to the case of improved nutrition. Students at the bottom end of the SAT scale are in general well above the intellectual median of the black population as a whole. And in any case, the improvement has taken place across the whole range of scores. So eager are the authors to persuade us that black gains are to be discounted that they encourage us not to place much weight on the fact that there was a 37 percent increase in the number of students scoring in the 600 range of the SAT from 1980 to 1990 [p. 722] because "so small a proportion of all black students were involved.")

WHY?

Let me be clear about what I am asserting about *The Bell Curve*'s treatment of evidence. For the question of genetic contribution to the IQ gap, almost all of the direct evidence has been left out, and the single study that is treated at any length is the only one consistent with a genetic component to the gap. Moreover, that study is presented without even its author's qualifications.

For the question of intervention, most of the relevant evidence has not been presented, and that which has is presented in a one-sidedly negative light that is far from the analysis that would be offered by most people who are familiar with the data.

For the question of convergence between black and white IQ, the authors have quite simply misdescribed the straightforward data on the question that they themselves present: A reduction in the B/W gap of between four and eight IQ points over the period preceding 1990 is described as possibly being as high as a two to three point reduction. Purportedly relevant data comparing the gap for mothers and children are misanalyzed.

Having distorted the evidence on the B/W gap in a variety of ways that would serve to persuade the uninformed reader that the gap was significantly genetic in origin, the authors magnanimously proclaim themselves to be "agnostic" on the genetic question. This has fooled many readers into accepting the authors' self-characterization as objective and fair-minded, but it is to be hoped that this pose is being unmasked and that it will soon be recognized by the scientific community that the authors' treatment of none of the three issues discussed here could be published in any respectable peer-reviewed journal.

The most benign interpretation of the missing, misdescribed, and oddly-interpreted evidence is that the authors were simply operating with outmoded psychological notions that make their treatment of the issues seem reasonable to them. The science reflected in the book is that of an old-fashioned psychometrics and an almost equally outdated behavior genetics that operate in hermetic isolation from recent findings about the biology of behavior and the modifiability of behavior given its underlying biology, from notions of evolution and cultural evolution, and from conceptions of economic, sociological, and social-psychological processes that might play a role in the development of particular sorts of cognitive skills. Virtually the only social fact that Herrnstein and Murray allow into their picture of the world would appear to be socioeconomic status. That this is no exaggeration is revealed by the following quotation: "Suppose that all the observed ethnic differences in tested intelligence originate in some mysterious environmental differences—mysterious, because we know from material already presented that socioeconomic factors cannot be much of the explanation" (p. 298).

It is deeply unfortunate that this narrow mentality is the one that is currently shaping the debate on the heritability of black-white differences in IQ. At least we can hope that the scientific community will recognize and communicate the omissions, misstatements, and eccentric interpretations that characterize this book and begin to reshape the debate.

NOTES

1. Scarr, S, & Weinberg, R. A. (1983). The Minnesota adoption studies: Genetic differences and malleability. *Child Development, 54,* 260–267.

2. Adolescent black and mixed race children seem to have had a very high level of emotional distress, with, at one point, more than half being in psychotherapy of one kind or another. Personal communication, Sandra Scarr, 1982.

3. Tizard, B., Cooperman, A., & Tizard, J. (1972). Environmental effects on language development: a study of young children in long-stay residential nurseries. *Child Development, 43,* 342–343.

4. Flynn, J. R. (1980). *Race, IQ, and Jensen.* London: Routledge and Kegan Paul, 110–111.

5. Flynn, J. R. (1980), 94.

6. Ibid., 87–88.

7. Scarr, S., Pakstis, S., Katz, H, & Barker, W. B. (1977). Absence of a relationship between degree of white ancestry and intellectual skills within a black population. *Human Genetics, 39,* 73–77 and 82–83.

8. Loehlin, J. D., Vandenberg, S. G., & Osborne, R. T. (1973). Blood-group genes and Negro-white ability differences. *Behavior Genetics, 3,* 263–270.

9. Witty, P. A., & Jenkins, M. D. (1934). The educational achievement of a group of gifted Negro children. *Journal of Educational Psychology, 25,* 586.

10. Willerman, L., Naylor, A. F., & Myrianthopoulos, N. C. (1974). Intellectual development of children from interracial matings: performance in infancy and at 4 years. *Behavior Genetics, 4,* 84–88.

11. Flynn, J. R. (1980), 180.

12. Smith, J. P. (1993). Racial and Ethnic Differences in Wealth Using the HRS, *Journal of Human Resources*, forthcoming.

13. Brooks-Gunn, J., Kebanov, P., & Duncan, G. J. (In press, *Child Development*).

14. Garber, H. L. (1988). *The Milwaukee project: Preventing mental retardation in children at risk*. Washington, D.C.: American Association on Mental Retardation.

15. Ramey, C. T. (1992). High-risk children and IQ: Altering intergenerational patterns. *Intelligence, 16,* 239–256.

16. Ramey, C. T., Bryant, D. M., Wasik, B. H., Sparling, J. J., Fendt, K. H., & LaVange, L. M. (1992). Infant health and development program for low birth weight, premature infants: Program elements, family participation, and child intelligence. *Pediatrics, 3,* 4343–465.

17. Ramey, S. L., & Ramey, C. T. (1992). Early educational intervention with disadvantaged children—to what effect? *Applied and Preventive Psychology, 1,* 131–140. Zigler, E. (1993). *Head Start and beyond* (New Haven: Yale University Press, 1993).

18. Bennett, W. J. (1987). *Schools that work*. Washington, D.C.: U.S. Department of Education.

19. Herrnstein, R. J., Nickerson, R. S., De Sanchez, M., & Swets, J. A. (1986). Teaching thinking skills. *American Psychologist, 41,* 1279–1289. Nickerson, R. S. (1986). Project intelligence: An account and some reflections. In *Facilitating development: International perspectives, programs, and practices*. M. Schwebel & C. A. Maher (Eds.). New York: Haworth Press.

20. Selvin, P. (1992). Math education: Multiplying the meager numbers. *Science, 258,* 1200–1201.

21. Treisman, U. (1992). Studying students studying calculus: A look at the lives of minority mathematics students in college. *The College Mathematics Journal, 23,* 362–372.

22. Steele, C. (1992). Race and the schooling of black Americans. *Atlantic Monthly* (April): 68ff.

23. Derek Neal, National Opinion Research Council, personal commu-

nication, January, 1995.

24. This would not be necessary if the mothers' and children's means were both 100 and the standard deviation fifteen. Under these circumstances, the test scores are already in standard score (standard deviation) form.

25. U.S. Department of Education. (1994). *NAEP trends in academic progress*. Washington D.C.; National Center for Education Statistics, 13.

26. The curves showing that there was trivial change for whites in both math and verbal SAT scores from 1980 to 1992—a period during which there were substantial gains for blacks—may be seen on page 425 of *The Bell Curve*.

27. The data that became available after those the authors report continue the worsening of the B/W gap. The gap for the past twenty-five years follows very closely the economic circumstances of blacks ten years or so prior to measurement. The period up to about 1975 was one of dramatic economic improvement. The period after 1980 has been one of slight reversal of economic gains. (U.S. Bureau of the Census, Public Use Microdata Samples form the censuses of 1940 to 1980 and the March 1988 Current Population Survey.)

28. College Board Reports. (1994). College-bound seniors: Profile reports (New York: College Entrance Exam Board and Educational Testing Service), iv.

The Sources of The Bell Curve

JEFFREY ROSEN AND CHARLES LANE

By scrutinizing the footnotes and bibliography in *The Bell Curve*, readers can more easily recognize the project for what it is: a chilly synthesis of the work of disreputable race theorists and eccentric eugenicists. "Here was a case of stumbling onto a subject that had all the allure of the forbidden," Charles Murray told the *New York Times*. "Some of the things we read to do this work, we literally hide when we're on planes and trains. We're furtively peering at this stuff."

It would be unfair, of course, to ascribe to Murray and Herrnstein all the noxious views of their sources. Mere association with dubious thinkers does not discredit the book by itself; and *The Bell Curve*, ultimately, must stand or fall on the rigor of its own arguments. But even a superficial examination of the primary sources suggests that some of Murray and Herrnstein's substantive arguments rely on questionable data and hotly contested scholarship, produced by academics whose ideological biases are pronounced. To this extent, important portions of the book must be treated with skepticism.

Much of *The Bell Curve*'s data purporting to establish an inherited difference in intelligence among blacks, whites, and Asians is drawn from the work of Richard Lynn of the University of Ulster. In the acknowledgments to *The Bell Curve*, Murray and Herrnstein say they "benefited especially from the advice" of Lynn, whom they refer to elliptically as "a scholar of racial and ethnic differences." Lynn is an associate editor of, and, since 1971, a frequent contributor to, *Mankind Quarterly*, a journal of racialist anthropology, founded by the Scottish white supremacist Robert Gayre. *Mankind Quarterly* has a long history of publishing pseudoscientific accounts of black inferiority. Lynn and others have used its pages to ventilate their view that society should foster the reproduction of the genetically superior, and discourage that of the genetically inferior.

Murray and Herrnstein rely most heavily on an article that Lynn published in *Mankind Quarterly* in 1991, "Race Differences in Intelligence: A Global Perspective." In the article, Lynn reviews what he calls the "world literature on racial differences in intelligence." He notes that "the first good study of the intelligence of pure African Negroids was carried out in South Africa" in 1929, without mentioning that this study was based on an administration of the now-discredited U.S. Army Beta Test. He also claims that the median IQ of black Africans is 70—based solely on a single test of blacks in South Africa in 1989. Murray and Herrnstein invoke this dubious figure, but they manage to confuse it: they say that the *median* black African IQ is 75.

Lynn concludes that "Mongoloids have the fastest reaction times," and the highest IQs, "followed by Caucasoids and then by Negroids." Indeed, Lynn, who specializes in "Oriental Intelligence," has also advanced the extraordinary claim that the average Japanese IQ score is ten points higher than that of the average European. This assertion, made in the pages of *Nature* in 1982, was refuted in a follow-up study conducted by Harold W. Stevenson of the University of Michigan. After examining what he calls "1,500 of the most important technological and scientific discoveries which have ever been made," Lynn reaches the following conclusion: "Who can doubt that the Caucasoid and the Mongoloid are the only two races that have made any significant contribution to civilization?"

Lynn has an exotic explanation for the racial differences he has purported to discover. As Murray and Herrnstein observe in a footnote, "Lynn explains the evolution of racial differences in intelligence in terms of the ancestral migrations of groups of early hominids from the relatively benign environments of Africa to the harsher and more demanding Eurasian latitudes, where they branched into the Caucasoids and Mongoloids." Similar theories, Murray and Herrnstein note without irony, "were not uncommon among anthropologists and biologists of a generation or two ago."

Murray and Herrnstein also introduce readers to the work of J. Phillipe Rushton, a Canadian psychologist. Rushton has argued that Asians are more intelligent than Caucasians, have larger brains for their body size, smaller penises, lower sex drive, are less fertile, work harder, and are more readily socialized; and Caucasians have the same relationship to blacks. In his most recent book, *Race, Evolution and Behavior*, Rushton acknowledges the assistance of Herrnstein; and Murray and Herrnstein return the compliment, devoting two pages of their own book to a defense of Rushton. Among the views that Herrnstein and Murray suggest Rushton has supported with "increasingly detailed and convincing empirical reports" is the theory that, in their words, "the average Mongoloid is toward one end of the continuum of reproductive strategies—the few offspring, high survival, and high parental investment end—the average Negroid is shifted toward the other end, and the average Caucasoid is in the middle."

In a gratuitous two-page appendix, Murray and Herrnstein go out of their way to say that "Rushton's work is not that of a crackpot or a bigot." But in an interview with *Rolling Stone*, Rushton colloquially summarized his research agenda: "Even if you take things like athletic ability or sexuality—not to reinforce stereotypes—but it's a trade-off: more brain or more penis. You can't have everything." And in a 1986 article in *Politics and Life Sciences*, Rushton suggested that Nazi Germany's military prowess was connected to the purity of its gene pool, and warned that egalitarian ideas endangered "North European civilization."

This, then, is the evolution of Murray and Herrnstein's data. The tradition which they benignly label "classicist" stretches back to the Victorian era, when Sir William Galton, the cousin of Darwin, argued that Africans were less intelligent and had slower "reaction times" than Englishmen; it extends through Charles Spearman, who argued that socially desirable traits, such as honesty and intelligence, could be measured together; and it was updated in 1969 by Arthur Jensen who relied on Galton's hundred-year-old estimates for his conclusion that blacks were less intelligent than whites.

In addition to appropriating the data of Spearman, Jensen, Lynn and Rushton, Murray and Herrnstein faithfully duplicate the analytical structure of their arguments. It is no coincidence, therefore, that Rushton's book includes the same strains of conservative multiculturalism that Murray embraced in his essay in *The New Republic*. Anticipating Murray's celebration of "clannish self-esteem," Rushton devotes an entire chapter of his book to a genetic explanation for ethnocentrism: "According to genetic similarity theory, people can be expected to favor their own group over others." And he speculates that "favoritism for one's own ethnic group may have arisen as an extension of enhancing family and social cohesiveness."

The Bell Curve, in short, is not an original or courageous book. It the work of a controversialist and popularizer of ideas from the fringes of the academy that have been repeatedly aired and repeatedly ignored. And despite the publicity that accompanied the publication of *The Bell Curve*, Murray's celebration of "clannish self-esteem" could hardly be more ineptly timed. The notion of American blacks and whites as increasingly culturally and genetically distinct "clans" seems especially implausible in an age when the healthy growth of ethnic intermarriage promises to undermine the concept of coherent racial classification entirely. It is not surprising to discover, after scratching the surface of Charles Murray's footnotes, the shabbiness of the scholarly tradition on which he has staked his reputation.

Paradise Miscalculated

DANTE RAMOS

If one psychological insight could tell us what to blame for our societal ills, we could stop agonizing. Science would identify a culprit and spell out where and how to intervene. With that purpose in mind, Charles Murray and Richard J. Herrnstein use the basic premise of psychometrics—that some people are measurably smarter than others—as a social philosopher's stone. And in their book *The Bell Curve* they argue that less intelligent people are identifiable through IQ tests, that IQ is hard to raise, and that the less intelligent are more prone to social pathologies than the more intelligent. Since low-IQ people are reproducing quickly, present trends will lead to a custodial state in which the shrinking productive classes resentfully fork over more and more money to feed a growing underclass. Murray and Herrnstein want to avert this disaster.

In sketching out an appropriate social vision, they subtly revise a principle that has surfaced and resurfaced, in one form or another, in Anglo-American political philosophy since *Leviathan:* Individuals are by nature equal as long as no one is strong enough to defeat all the others combined, and they remain equal for the purposes of the state.[1] Murray and Herrnstein ask Americans and our government to reject the notion that one individual can function in the world as well as any other and instead to take account of intellectual variation.[2] Since affirmative action won't help them catch up to whites, members of low-IQ ethnic groups should take a clannish pride that their collective genius lies in nonintellectual matters. Government should abolish programs that, like Aid to Families with Dependent Children, subsidize childbirth among the poor and stupid and return the responsibility for welfare services to communities. Educational resources should be diverted from the uneducable toward the gifted.

It's an odd utopia, but then again this is a book in which the *Federalist Papers* are transmogrified into just another study—"Hamilton et al. 1787." Still, their ideas are defensible as long as they haven't papered over inconvenient facts and common sense. What happens if Murray and Herrnstein, in their effort to turn psychology into political and social theory, have overstated their case?

Murray, at least, ought to be the last writer to fall into that trap. After all, he became famous for the book *Losing Ground,* in which he embraced the plain meaning of data that backed up what jaded welfare caseworkers have claimed for years: many forms of public assistance can destroy at least some individuals' incentives to work,[3] Declaring that "when [welfare] reforms finally do occur, they will happen not because stingy people have won, but because generous people have stopped kidding themselves," Murray acidically condemned liberals for believing that the poor were everywhere and always helpless victims—and for ignoring evidence that would contradict this prefabricated view.[4] Yet a careful scan of *The Bell Curve*'s main text and of the discussion in the endnotes and appendices turns up too much important counter-evidence relegated to endnotes, too much tendentious data interpretation, and too many not-quite-credible studies.

This cripples their case, since how much you fear the custodial state depends entirely on your confidence in their science. But the interpretive slip-ups begin at the front end of the argument, when Murray and Herrnstein try to prove definitively that IQ scores matter—in other words, that intelligence remains stable over time and that low-intelligence individuals can be identified through tests. They dismiss anecdotal evidence that schools can raise IQ scores for disadvantaged children, and they cite newspaper articles indicating that one alleged success story actually resulted from school employees who let students cheat.[5] Of course, these articles speak nothing about the environmentally deprived, for several hundred pages later, in the note, you learn that this sorry event occurred in Fairfax County, Virginia—the wealthiest county in America.[6]

Murray and Herrnstein aren't entirely convincing about the reliability of IQ tests, either. An otherwise intelligent individual might well choke on standardized examinations, in which case earnings, occupation, and productivity—"all the important measures of success"—would have little correlation with IQ scores.[7] Murray and Herrnstein line up evidence that IQ is a reasonable predictor of success. Yet studies they raise in unrelated discussions suggest a different conclusion. In one study of Marines in technical jobs, after a year on the job low-IQ workers performed worse than high-IQ workers on tests of job knowledge—but their performance as judged by work samples was just as good.[8] According to other studies, there are proportionally far more blacks than whites in high-IQ occupations like law and medicine when blacks' relatively lower IQs are taken into account; Murray and Herrnstein cite this as an argument against affirmative action, but another reasonable possibility is that IQ tests underestimate some individuals'—in this case, many blacks'—cognitive ability.[9]

Suppose that the tests are reliable. Low IQ still only becomes a social problem when it correlates highly with such undesirables as divorce, illegitimacy, and—most importantly—welfare dependency. But even to readers who make it through the data appendices, Murray and Herrnstein dissemble about how poorly IQ (and parental socioeconomic status as well) predicts these phenomena. In the explanatory text, they suggest that an analysis in which IQ, parental SES and age together explain 17 percent of the variation in the incidence of a given phenomenon is one of their least compelling ones.[10] This is blatantly false. From the ensuing pages it becomes obvious that in other analyses—which figure prominently in the main text—the three predictors together account for as little as 3.14 percent, 2.76 percent or 0.76 percent.

The verbal argument is no more convincing. Since, by definition, underclass behavior is characterized by chronic welfare dependency, Murray and Herrnstein are right to investigate its relationship—not just the relationship of welfare dependency in general—to IQ. But since chronic recipients and occasional recipients show about the same mean IQ, and since low parental SES constitutes by their calculations a greater risk for chronic recipiency than IQ does, they suddenly decide that the sample of respondents is too restricted for them to draw conclusions.[11]

Murray and Herrnstein also need to prove significant dysgenic pressure. In other words, the mean IQ of the population must be falling at a considerable rate. Fortunately, the speeds that their data suggest are either too small to be worrisome or too large to be believed. One study drawn partially from census figures concludes that the mean IQ of American mothers is approximately 98; yet because the researcher used so rough an estimation procedure and because male scores on IQ tests usually exceed female scores by one or two points, it's hard to separate any bona fide dysgenic pressure from statistical noise.[12] On the other hand, using a different database Murray and Herrnstein estimate that 10 percent of the children of white mothers and 33 percent of the children of black mothers with IQs of 100 have IQs below 80. These numbers imply that white mean IQ remains constant over time, but also that black mean IQ plunges by an astounding 13.5 points per generation.[13] Implausible, yet this conclusion follows necessarily from calculations Murray and Herrnstein have performed themselves and appear to trust.

Of course, it's their precisely their analysis of cognitive differences among races that looks most suspicious. They raise and dismiss analyses that say tests can be valid within ethnic groups but not across ethnic groups. One such analysis is John Ogbu's distinction among autonomous, immigrant, and castelike minorities; the third type, Ogbu suggests, score low on all measures of educational achievement because of intense discrimination.[14] Social psychologist Jeff Hammond and physician Ray Howard have suggested a mechanism: expectations of failure hamper intellectual competition, and by extension general intellectual development, among blacks.[15] Clearly Murray and Herrnstein introduce Ogbu's theory as another pious hypothesis easily punctured by reality.

But the authors' choice of contrary data is bizarre. While the black IQ mean of 85 falls far below the average for whites, black Africans, who suffer from no caste status, have an average IQ of at most 75.[16] Think about what this means. If black African IQs are distributed in a bell curve similar to that among Americans, African blacks with the same intelligence as an average American are outnumbered by moderately retarded African blacks. A clinical description of individuals with IQs of 50 underlines the absurdity: a standard pediatric textbook helpfully notes, "Those who are well adjusted may be able to function semi-independently in supervised living and sheltered workshop settings."[17] A substantial proportion of the African populace would be unable to care for itself, not just economically but in the routines of everyday life. We ought to question whether Murray and Herrnstein's zeal to attack affirmative action has besmirched at least the interpretation and possibly the data themselves.

Even a full catalogue of their tortured empirics might not refute *The Bell Curve*'s descriptive chapters, and it wouldn't pretend to. It would, however, cast doubt upon the ability of Murray and Herrnstein to measure the speed with which the United States is careening toward the apocalypse or, indeed, whether we're careening anywhere at all. That their book often seems factually slippery raises the possibility that their solutions to the intelligence crisis, however severe it is, may be at once philosophically unkind and impotent in practice.

They answer generally that Americans should accept natural inequality as a given while using dysgenic potential as a yardstick for social policies. This takes several specific forms. One of these is the clan pride that amounts to a nondysgenic palliative to blacks saddened by their inferior intelligence. It is a perfectly destructive recommendation, whether the postulated racial differences in cognitive ability are environmental or mostly genetic in origin. The caste theory explains why the difference between environmental and genetic factors *do* matter deeply. If the genetic component of the measured black-white difference is substantial, the environmental component is still large; a clan pride based upon revering entertainers and athletes and rejecting intellectual role models—who needs Charles Darwin when you've got Chuck D?—would only increase the environment-based differential. (If you consider how the existence of genetic differences would intensify caste status, the environmental piece would grow even more.) If the genetic component is small, Murray and Herrnstein's conservative multiculturalism would make the black-white difference skyrocket. Their cultural construct would produce more perverse effects than the worst work disincentive ever devised. Talk about losing ground.

It turns out that another key suggestion, that education funds be redirected away from the low end of the IQ distribution and toward gifted students, cannot be justified—at least not with the facts presented in *The Bell Curve*. When Murray and Herrnstein assert that "it may be within the capability of an education system—probably with the complicity of broader social trends—to put a ceiling on, or actually dampen, the realized intelligence of those with high potential," their suggestion seems curious, since they spend the first seventeen chapters of their book denying the existence of a "potential intelligence" not picked up by tests.[18] Besides, none of the studies cited in their discussion of the dumbed-down curricula or of the lack of funds for gifted education suggests any causal link to dampened intelligence.[19] Moreover, they concede, deep within the supplemental matter of their book, that not having a high school diploma is a better predictor of welfare dependency, "over and above the effects of either cognitive ability or socioeconomic background."[20] Surely spending money to keep at-risk young women in high school is nothing to scoff at, even when the alternative is to make a superhuman out of an overachiever.

This particular choice illustrates the impossible position of a state that views all of its citizens as equal under the law but views some as less functional than others in a meaningful, scientifically proven, even genetically determined way. As long as the state has any explicit or implicit social policies—and Murray and Herrnstein signal no objection to it doing so—there will always be choices calculated not in terms of costs and benefits or right and wrong, but in terms of superior people and inferior people.

More circumspect advocates of Murray and Herrnstein's plan would take fuller account of the costs of these reforms. After all, the costs of enshrining inequality into policy are not merely moral ones. While Murray and Herrnstein occupy themselves with estimates of the drag affirmative action and antidiscrimination laws impose upon the American economy, they ignore Chicago economist Gary S. Becker's classic work *The Economics of Discrimination*. Becker demonstrates that when one group indulges its taste to discriminate against another it drives up the cost of doing business, and anything that increases that taste will drive costs up more.[21] When they talk about eliminating public aid, they don't pause to ask whether children whose neighborhoods don't provide enough for them will have IQs any higher than those of poor children now. You begin to wonder whether Murray and Herrnstein understand that, when social science is transformed into a social blueprint, empirical imprecision has political consequences.

But the last thing social-science totalists are inclined to do is to contemplate the damage that their own errors might cause. Early on in their attempt to deny any meaningful equality, Murray and Herrnstein include a scatterplot of education charted against income, and the correlation is a thin +.33. They warn, "Throughout the rest of the book, keep [this] figure in mind, for it is what a highly significant correlation in the social sciences look like."[22] If true, then social scientists should not let themselves thunder general statements about cause and effect. They should not let themselves base a blueprint for society entirely upon empirical evidence, since all of their findings will be contested and many will be scaled back or refuted. And, most of all, they should not let themselves assert that improving life for the poor and dispossessed is as impossible as urging rain to fall upward.

NOTES

1. Charles Murray and Richard J. Herrnstein, "Race, Genes and IQ—An Apologia," *The New Republic*, October 31, 1994: 35–37. Thomas Hobbes, *Leviathan*, chaps. xiii (1-3), xiv (18), xv (21-23), xvii (13-15), xxx (16).

2. Herrnstein and Murray, *The Bell Curve* (New York: The Free Press, 1994), 484.

3. Murray, *Losing Ground: American Social Policy 1950–1980* (New York: Basic Books, 1984), 154–191.

4. Ibid., 236.

5. Herrnstein and Murray, 399.

6. Ibid., 743n36. U.S. Bureau of the Census, *County and City Data Book: 1994* (Washington, D.C.: U.S. Government Printing Office, 1994), xv.

7. Ibid., 13.

8. Ibid., 80.

9. Ibid., 321.

10. Ibid., 594.

11. Ibid., 199.

12. Ibid., 350; 735n35; 275.

13. Ibid., 337. An IQ of 80 falls about 1.3 standard deviations from the overall mean and represents the tenth centile of the overall distribution. If 10 percent of the white children fall within the first ten centiles of the white IQ distribution, a mean of 100 is implied. The 33rd centile mark (which in the implied black distribution is 80 in absolute terms) falls at about 0.4 standard deviation below the mean. Since the distance between the white mean and the 80 mark in the distribution is the sum of the distance between the black and white means and the distance between the black mean and the 80 mark, the implied difference between the black and white means is 0.9 standard deviation, or 13.5 IQ points.

14. Ibid., 307.

15. Jeff Howard and Ray Hammond, "Rumors of Inferiority," *The New Republic*, September 9, 1985, 17–21.

16. Herrnstein and Murray, 239.

17. Jack P. Shankoff, "Mental Retardation," in Richard E. Behrmann, ed., *Nelson Textbook of Pediatrics*, 14th ed. (Philadelphia: W. B. Saunders–Harcourt Brace Jovanovich, 1992), 96.

18. Herrnstein and Murray, 427.

19. Ibid., 427–435; 751–753nn31–50.

20. Ibid., 704n14.

21. Gary S. Becker, *The Economics of Discrimination,* 2nd ed., (Chicago: University of Chicago, 1971), passim.

22. Herrnstein and Murray, 67.

Ethnicity and IQ

THOMAS SOWELL

The Bell Curve is a very sober, very thorough, and very honest book—on a subject where sobriety, thoroughness, and honesty are only likely to provoke cries of outrage. Its authors, Charles Murray and the late Professor Richard J. Herrnstein of Harvard, must have known that writing about differences in intelligence would provoke shrill denunciations from some quarters. But they may not have expected quite so many, quite so loudly, and/or quite so venomously, and from such a wide spectrum of people who should know better.

The great danger in this emotional atmosphere is that there will develop a two-tier set of reactions—violent public outcries against the message of *The Bell Curve* by some and uncritical private acceptance of it by many others, who hear no rational arguments being used against it. Both reactions are unwarranted, but not unprecedented, in the over-heated environment surrounding so many touchy social issues today.

The predictive validity and social implications of intelligence test results are carefully explored by Herrnstein and Murray in more than 500 pages of text plus another 300 pages of appendices, footnotes, and an index. *The Bell Curve* is an education on the whole subject, including the evidence pro and con on a wide variety of controversial issues. Even where the authors clearly come down on one side of a given issue, they usually present the case for believing otherwise. In such candor, as well as in the clarity with which technical issues are discussed without needless jargon, this book is a model that others might well emulate.

Contrary to much hysteria in the media, this is not a book about race, nor is it trying to prove that blacks are capable only of being hewers of wood and drawers of water. The first twelve chapters of the book deal solely with data from all-white samples, so as to be rid of the whole distracting issue of racial differences in IQ scores. In these chapters, Herrnstein and Murray establish their basic case that intelligence test scores are highly correlated with many important social phenomena, ranging from academic success to infant mortality, which is far higher among babies whose mothers are in the bottom quarter of the IQ distribution.

Empirical data from a wide variety of sources establish that even the differing educational backgrounds or socioeconomic levels of the families in which individuals were raised are not as good as predictors of future income, academic success, job performance ratings, or even rates of divorce, as IQ scores are. It is not that IQ results are infallible, or even that correlations between IQ and these other social phenomena are high. Rather, the correlations simply tend to be higher than correlations involving other factors which might seem on the surface to be more relevant.

Even in nonintellectual occupations, pen-and-paper tests of general mental ability produce higher correlations with future job performance than do "practical" tests of the particular skills involved in these jobs.

In such a comprehensive study of IQ scores and their social implications, there was no way to leave out questions of intergroup differences in IQ without the absence of such a discussion being glaring evidence of moral cowardice. After ignoring this issue for the first twelve chapters, Herrnstein and Murray enter into a discussion of it in chapter 13 ("Ethnic Differences in Cognitive Ability"), not as zealots making a case but as people laying out the issues and reaching the conclusions which seem to them most consistent with the facts—while also presenting the case for alternative explanations. They conclude that the apparent influence of biological inheritance on IQ score differences among members of the general society seem also to explain IQ differences between different racial and ethnic groups.

This is what set off the name-calling and mud-slinging with which so many critics of *The Bell Curve* have responded. Such responses, especially among black intellectuals and "leaders," are only likely to provoke others to conclude that they protesteth too much, lending more credence to the conclusion that genetics determines intelligence. Such a conclusion goes beyond what Herrnstein and Murray said and much beyond what the facts will support.

First of all, Herrnstein and Murray make a clear distinction between saying that IQ is genetically inheritable among individuals in general and saying that the differences among particular groups are due to their different genetic inheritances. They say further that this whole issue is "still riddled with more questions than answers." They caution against "taking the current ethnic differences as etched in stone." But none of this saves them from the wrath of those who promote the more "politically correct" view that the tests are culturally biased and lack predictive validity for nonwhite minorities.

It is an anomaly that there should even be a controversy over the predictive validity of tests. The question of predictive validity is ultimately an empirical question—and on this there is a vast amount of data going back many years. Herrnstein and Murray are only summarizing these data when they shoot down the arguments and evasions by which the conventional wisdom tries to say that tests do not accurately predict future performances, whether in academia, in job performance, or in any other field of human endeavor. Long before *The Bell Curve* was published, the empirical literature showed repeatedly that IQ and other mental tests do not predict a lower subsequent performance for minorities than the performance that in fact emerges. In terms of logic and evidence, the predictive validity of mental tests is the issue least open to debate. On this, Murray and Herrnstein are most clearly and completely correct.

In thus demolishing the foundation underlying such practices as double standards in college admissions and "race-norming" of employment tests, *The Bell Curve* threatens a whole generation of social policies and the careers of those who promote such policies. To those committed to these policies, this may be at least as bad as the authors remaining "agnostic" (as Herrnstein and Murray put it) on the question as to whether black-white IQ differences are genetic in origin.

On some other issues, the arguments and conclusions of *The Bell Curve* are much more open to dispute. Yet critics have largely overlooked these disputable points, while concentrating their attacks on either the unassailable conclusions of the book or the presumed bad intentions of the authors.

While Herrnstein and Murray do an excellent job of exposing the flaws in the argument that tests are "culturally biased" by showing that the greatest black-white differences are not on the questions which presuppose a middle-class vocabulary or middle-class experiences but on abstract questions, such as spatial-perceptual ability, their conclusion that this "phenomenon seems peculiarly concentrated in comparisons of ethnic groups" is simply wrong.

When European immigrant groups in the United States scored below the national average on mental tests, they scored lowest on the abstract parts of such tests. So did white mountaineer children in the United States tested back in the early 1930s. So did canal boat children in Britain, and so did rural British children compared to their urban counterparts, at a time before Britain had any significant nonwhite population. So did Gaelic-speaking children as compared to English-speaking children in the Hebrides Islands. This is neither a racial nor an ethnic peculiarity. It is a characteristic found among low-scoring groups of European as well as African ancestry.

In short, groups outside the cultural mainstream of contemporary Western society tend to do their worst on abstract questions, whatever their race might be. But to call this cultural "bias" is misleading, particularly if it suggests that these groups' "real" ability will produce better results than their test scores would indicate. That non sequitur was destroyed empirically long before Herrnstein and Murray sat down to write *The Bell Curve*. Whatever innate potential various groups may have, what they actually do will be done within some particular culture. That intractable reality cannot be circumvented by devising "culture-free" tests, for such tests would also be purpose-free in a world where there is no culture-free society.

Perhaps the strongest evidence against a genetic basis for intergroup differences in IQ is that the average level of mental test performance has changed very significantly for whole populations over time and, moreover, particular ethnic groups within the population have changed their relative positions during a period when there was very little intermarriage to change the genetic makeup of these groups.

While *The Bell Curve* cites the work of James R. Flynn, who found substantial increases in mental test performances from one generation to the next in a number of countries around the world, they seem not to acknowledge the devastating implications of that finding for the genetic theory of intergroup differences or for their own reiteration of long-standing claims that the higher fertility of low-IQ groups implies a declining national IQ level. Whatever the logic of that argument, ultimately this too is an empirical issue—and empirical evidence has likewise refuted the claim that IQ test performance would decline over time.

Even before Professor Flynn's studies, mental test results from American soldiers tested in World War II showed that their performances on these tests were higher than the performances of American soldiers in World War I by the equivalent of about twelve IQ points.

Perhaps the most dramatic changes were those in the mental test performances of Jews in the United States. The results of World War I mental tests conducted among American soldiers born in Russia—the great majority of whom were Jews—showed such low scores as to cause Carl Brigham, creator of the Scholastic Aptitude Test, to declare that these results "disprove the popular belief that the Jew is highly intelligent." Within a decade, however, Jews in the United States were scoring above the national average on mental tests and the data in *The Bell Curve* indicate that they are now far above the national average in IQ

Strangely, Herrnstein and Murray refer to "folklore" that "Jews and other immigrant groups were thought to be below average in intelligence." It was neither folklore nor anything as subjective as thoughts. It was based on hard data, as hard as any data in *The Bell Curve*. These groups repeatedly tested below average on the mental tests of the World War I era, both in the army and in civilian life. For Jews, it is clear that later tests showed radically different results—during an era when there was very little intermarriage to change the genetic makeup of American Jews.

My own research of twenty years ago showed that the IQs of

both Italian Americans and Polish Americans also rose substantially over a period of decades. Unfortunately, there are many statistical problems with these particular data, growing out of the conditions under which they were collected. However, while my data could never be used to compare the IQs of Polish and Italian children, whose IQ scores came from different schools, nevertheless the close similarity of their general patterns of rising IQ scores over time seems indicative—especially since it follows the rising patterns found among Jews and among American soldiers in general between the two world wars, as well as rising IQ scores in other countries around the world.

The implications of such rising patterns of mental test performance is devastating to the central hypothesis of those who have long expressed the same fear as Herrnstein and Murray, that the greater fertility of low-IQ groups would lower the national (and international) IQ over time. The logic of their argument is so clear and compelling that the directly opposite empirical result should be considered a refutation of the assumptions behind that logic.

One of the reasons why widespread improvements in results on IQ tests have received such little attention is that these tests have been normed to produce an average IQ of 100, regardless of how many questions are answered correctly. Like "race-norming" today, such generation-norming, as it were, produces a wholly fictitious equality concealing very real and very consequential differences. If a man who scores 100 on an IQ test today is answering more questions correctly than his grandfather with the same IQ answered two generations ago, then someone else who answers the same number of questions correctly today as this man's grandfather answered two generations ago may have an IQ of 85.

Herrnstein and Murray openly acknowledge this fact and christen it "the Flynn effect," in honor of Professor Flynn who discovered it. But they seem not to see how crucially it undermines the case for a genetic explanation of interracial IQ differences. They say:

The national averages have in fact changed by amounts that are comparable to the fifteen or so IQ points separating blacks and whites in America. To put it another way, on the average, whites today differ from whites, say, two generations ago as much as whites today differ from blacks today. Given their size and speed, the shifts in time necessarily have been due more to changes in the environment than to changes in the genes.

While this open presentation of evidence against the genetic basis of interracial IQ differences is admirable, the failure to draw the logical inference seems puzzling. Blacks today are just as racially different from whites of two generations ago as they are from whites today. Yet the data suggest that the number of questions that blacks answer correctly on IQ tests today is very similar to the number answered correctly by past generations of whites. If race A differs from race B in IQ and two generations of race A differ from each other by the same amount, where is the logic in suggesting that the IQ differences are racial, even partially?

Herrnstein and Murray do not address this question but instead shift to public policy discussion:

> Couldn't the mean of blacks move 15 points as well through environmental changes? There seems no reason why not—but also no reason to believe that white and Asian means can be made to stand still while the Flynn effect works its magic.

But the issue is not solely one of either predicting or controlling the future. It is a question of the validity of the conclusion that differences between genetically different groups are due to those genetic differences, whether in whole or in part. When any factor differs as much from A_1 to A_2 as it does from A_2 to B_2, how can one conclude that this factor is due to the difference between A in general and B in general? That possibility is not precluded by the evidence,[1] but neither does the evidence point in that direction.

A remarkable phenomenon commented on in the Moynihan Report of thirty years ago goes unnoticed in *The Bell Curve*—the prevalence of females among blacks who score high on mental tests. Others who have done studies of high-IQ blacks have found several times as many females as males above the 120 IQ level. Since black males and black females have the same genetic inheritance, this substantial disparity must have some other roots, especially since it is not found in studies of high-IQ individuals in the general society, such as the famous Terman studies of high-IQ children, which followed these children on into adulthood and later life. If IQ differences of this magnitude can occur with no genetic difference at all, then it is more than mere speculation to say that some unusual environmental effects must be at work among blacks. However, these environmental effects need not be limited to blacks, for other low-IQ groups of European or other ancestries have likewise tended to have females over-represented among their higher scorers, even though the Terman studies of high-IQ individuals from the general population found no such patterns. One possibility is that females are more resistant to bad environmental conditions, as some other studies suggest. In any event, large sexual disparities in high-IQ individuals where there are no genetic—or socioeconomic—differences present a challenge to both the Herrnstein-Murray thesis and to most of their critics.

Black males and black females are not the only groups with significant IQ differences without any genetic differences. Identical twins with significantly different birth weights also have IQ differences, with the heavier twin averaging nearly nine points higher IQ than the lighter one in some studies.[2] This effect is not found where the lighter twin weighs at least six and a half pounds, suggesting that deprivation of nutrition must reach some threshold level before it has a permanent effect on the brain during its crucial early development.

Perhaps the most troubling aspect of *The Bell Curve* from an intellectual standpoint is its authors' uncritical approach to statistical correlations. One of the first things taught in introductory statistics is that correlation is not causation. It is also one of the first things forgotten and one of the most widely ignored facts in public policy research. The statistical term "multicollinearity," dealing with spurious correlations, appears only once in this massive book.

Multicollinearity refers to the fact that many variables are highly correlated with one another, so that it is very easy to believe that a certain result comes from variable A, when in fact it is due to variable Z, with which A happens to be correlated. In real life, innumerable factors go together. An example I liked to use in class when teaching economics involved a study showing that economists with only a bachelor's degree had higher incomes than economists with a master's degree and these in turn had higher incomes than economists with Ph.Ds. The clear suggestion that more education in economics leads to lower incomes would lead me to speculate as to how much money it was costing a student just to be enrolled in my course. In this case, when other variables that were readily available were taken into account, these spurious correlations disappeared.[3] In many other cases, however, other variables such as cultural influences cannot even be quantified, much less have their effects tested statistically.

The Bell Curve is really three books in one. It is a study of the general effects of IQ levels on the behavior and performance of people in general in a wide range of endeavors. Here it is on its most solid ground. It is also an attempt to understand the causes and social implications of IQ differences among ethnic groups. Here it is much more successful in analyzing the social implications where, as the authors say, "it matters little whether the genes are involved at all." Finally, it is a statement of grave concerns for the future of American society and a set of proposals as to how public policy should proceed in matters of education and social welfare programs. These concerns need voicing, even if they are not always compelling. One chance in five of disaster is not to be ignored. That is, after all, greater than the chance of disaster in playing Russian roulette.

In one sense, the issues are too important to ignore. In another sense the differences between what Herrnstein and Murray said and what others believe is much smaller than the latter seem to think. The notion that "genes are destiny" is one found among some of the more shrill critics but not in The Bell Curve itself. Nor do Herrnstein and Murray treat race as some kind of intellectual glass ceiling for individuals. As the authors say on page 278: "It should be no surprise to see (as one does every day) blacks functioning at high levels in every intellectually challenging field."

Critics who insist on arguing as if we are talking about an intellectual glass ceiling should recognize that this is their own straw man, not something from *The Bell Curve*. And if they refuse to recognize it, then we should recognize these critics as demagogues in the business of scavenging for grievances. *The Bell Curve* deserves critical attention, not public smearing and uncritical private acceptance.

NOTES

1. It is widely acknowledged that height is heavily influenced by genes and it is not controversial that races differ in height because of these genetic differences. Yet predictions of a decline in national height over time, because of a greater fertility in groups of shorter stature were likewise confounded by an increase in the national height. Yet, rightly, no one regards this as a refutation of the belief that heights are greatly influenced by genes and differ from race to race for genetic reasons. Rising IQs over time similarly do not refute the belief that races differ in IQ for genetic reasons, though it ought to at least raise a question about that belief. The parallel breaks down when we realize that heights can be measured directly, as innate potential cannot be, but is wholly dependent on inferences about what would have happened in the absence of environmental differences.

2. Miles D. Storfer, *Intelligence and Giftedness: The Contributions of Heredity and Early Environment* (San Francisco: Jossey-Bass Publishers, 1990), 13.

3. Because postgraduate degrees are usually required to be an economist, those economists with only a bachelor's degree tended to have entered the profession before such requirements became common. That is, they tended to be older and have more experience, with this experience being more likely to have been in the more lucrative business world rather than in academia.

Back to the Future with The Bell Curve: *Jim Crow, Slavery, and* G

JACQUELINE JONES

According to Richard Herrnstein and Charles Murray, we live in an age and a country untainted by history, an age that springs full blown from *g*, or the "general intelligence" of the citizens who live here, now. In presenting their rigidly deterministic view that IQ is the major force shaping social structure in the United States today, the authors of *The Bell Curve* exude a smug complacency about late twentieth-century American society: they argue that, judging from current housing and job patterns, people are pretty much where they should be—members of the so-called "cognitive elite" are ensconced in the wealthiest communities, while the poor (dubbed the "dull" or "very dull") languish, and deservedly so, in run-down, crime-ridden neighborhoods because they are unable to do any better for themselves. Yet even as the authors revel in the purity of a *g*-driven society, they hearken back to the supposedly glorious days of yesteryear, when poor people not only remained in their place, but also knew and understood that to be their place. As we read *The Bell Curve*, then, the past unfolds behind us, and beckons, full of promise for the future.

Among the more ludicrous claims of *The Bell Curve* is the authors' assertion that they are fearless scholars, venturing "into forbidden territory" (p. 10), into an intellectual no-man's land "between public discussion and private opinion" (p. 297). In fact, of course, the book is simply the most recent in a long line of efforts to prove the congenital inferiority of poor people in general, and (in this country) black people in particular. In the seventeenth century, settlers in the British colonies justified the enslavement of Africans because (most) blacks were non-Christian, non-English, and non-white. In the eighteenth century, white elites proposed that this particular group of poor people be permanently stigmatized, and forced to toil at the dirtiest jobs, so that white men could enjoy their republican liberties. In the late nineteenth century, southern politicians and landowners charged that the former slaves were lazy, immoral, and irresponsible; the federal government gave its blessing to efforts to keep black men and women disenfranchised, hard at work, and segregated from whites in schools and other public places. In the early twentieth century, racists turned to scientific theories to bolster their contention that whites were superior to non-whites in culture and intelligence.

As a text revealing of our times, then, *The Bell Curve* pursues traditional ends via new means; it seeks to denigrate blacks and justify their exclusion from the best jobs that the country has to offer. Well-paying, secure positions that include benefits like health care will remain the province of whites (and a few Asians), while the most menial jobs will remain reserved for blacks and the "New Immigrants" from Latin American countries. According to *The Bell Curve*, persistent racial and class segregation of neighborhoods and workplaces will insure that the poor, with their bad morals and shiftless ways, will not contaminate the well-to-do. As a political program, these ideas have the added advantage of appealing to poor whites, who might otherwise have to compete with the darker-skinned "lower orders" for scarce resources. From the perspective of an American historian, it is an old story, now told with a new set of "evidence" in the form of lots of picture-perfect regression analyses.

Beginning with a core assumption—that intelligence can be quantified, and that a single number encapsulates the potential of any individual—the authors make a number of claims about the social structure of the United States in the late twentieth century For example, they suggest that, generally speaking, an individual's job status reflects his or her IQ (p. 52); that the nation's public school system works well, and funnels bright children into the

appropriate channels of higher education (p. 104), as revealed by
the fact that all of the people who deserve to go to college (and a
number of black people who don't) are going (pp. 91–92). The collective stupidity (that is, low IQ) of a group is the cause of many
social problems suffered by its members—poverty (p.140–41) and
ill health among them (it is possible that "less intelligent people are
more accident prone" [p. 155]; hence presumably the folly of preventive medical care). Among the implicit policy recommendations
contained in *The Bell Curve* (the authors' disingenuous disclaimers
to the contrary notwithstanding) are the sterilization of all poor
women (because they are the agents of dysgenesis—defined as
"demographic trends. . . exerting downward pressures on the distribution of cognitive ability in the United States. . . pressures [that]
are strong enough to have social consequences" [p. 342]—and only
eugenesis will reverse this process); and disenfranchisement of certain groups in the population on the basis of IQ (because dumb
people make bad citizens).

In terms of the ways we as a nation sort out the rights and
responsibilities of individuals and groups, the American historical
trajectory follows a regressive path, according to Herrnstein and
Murray. Although the authors do not dwell explicitly on the alleged
glories of days gone by, they do seem to envision a society that
bears a striking resemblance to earlier periods in the nation's history, periods characterized by the legal and economic subordination
of black people as a group. Indeed, the history-minded reader can
discern that *The Bell Curve* begins by evoking the days of Jim Crow,
and then moves back to the time of slavery, building toward a dramatic climax in the last chapter, when the authors wax eloquent
about the virtues of the political ideology and social structure characteristic of the late eighteenth century.

As a blueprint for the good society, the period 1890 to 1915 has
much to recommend it when viewed from the perspective of *The
Bell Curve*. (Not coincidentally, it was during these years that intelligence testing came into vogue, no doubt in response to large-scale
immigration from Eastern Europe; economic transformations often
provoke new theories and systems of social control and racial inferiority.) During the late nineteenth and early twentieth centuries, the

executive branch, Congress, and the Supreme Court sanctioned a system of racial segregation in public places and institutions. While the country was undergoing a process of urbanization and industrialization, the vast majority of black people were domestic servants and agricultural workers (that is, they worked at jobs befitting their low mental abilities, in the parlance of *The Bell Curve*). Judging from Herrnstein and Murray's overall conclusions, we can speculate that this must have been a Golden Age in American history, since even mentally deficient people found a productive place in a dynamic, growing society; "in a simpler America, being comparatively low in the qualities measured by IQ did not necessarily affect the ability to find a valued niche in society. Many such people worked on farms" (p. 536).

Though obviously ignorant of the far reaching value of IQ testing, the cognitive elite in the Jim Crow South (perhaps intuitively) recognized the folly of funding schools for black children; therefore, tax money for education was routinely diverted away from blacks schools and given to white ones. Around the turn of the century, the southern public-education system (such as it was) reflected a racial division of labor that limited African Americans to work in the fields. For example, in 1900, fully 80 percent of Mississippi's black population were confined to agricultural labor, and another 15 percent to domestic service. In 1899, the state's governor, James K. Vardaman, observed, "people talk about elevating the race by education! It is not only folly, but it comes pretty nearly being [sic] criminal folly. . . . It is money thrown away." Foreshadowing *The Bell Curve*'s lament that too many black folks today are getting educational credentials they don't deserve, creating all sorts of unrealistic expectations, Vardaman was of the opinion that "literary education—the knowledge of books—does not seem to produce any substantial results with the negro, but serves rather to sharpen his cunning, breeds hopes that cannot be gratified, creates an inclination to avoid honest labor."

In the late nineteenth century, the rural South abided by a racial etiquette characterized by a superficial familiarity between members of the two races. And in order to do well—to buy land or obtain credit—individual blacks often had to look to a white patron, usually a man who could vouch for their honesty and testify to their hat-in-hand industry. Similarly, the authors of *The Bell Curve* suggest that a strict racial division of labor need not lead to hard feelings between individuals: *"We cannot think of a legitimate argument why any encounter between individual whites and blacks need be affected by the knowledge that an aggregate ethnic difference in measured intelligence is genetic instead of environmental"* (p. 313). In other words, there is no reason why a white lawyer need not engage in friendly banter with the custodian who cleans his office late at night; in the South, such easy familiarity was attributed to "good breeding" among whites. *The Bell Curve* similarly attests to the beneficial social effects of "good breeding."

The rural South, in a "simpler" America, was a time and place where "the community provided clear and understandable incentives for doing what needed to be done" (p. 537), characteristics attributed by Herrnstein and Murray to a society superior to our own. Jim Crow courts often deferred to Judge Lynch in dealing with black men and women who resisted doing "what needed to be done." The authors in fact suggest explicitly that they yearn for "a society where the rules about crimes are simple and the consequences are equally simple. Someone who commits a crime is probably caught—and almost certainly punished. The punishment almost certainly hurts (it is meaningful). Punishment follows arrest quickly, within a matter of days or weeks" (p. 543). Those were the days, when lynch mobs stood ready to act as the efficient agents of the cognitive elite. Thus Jim Crow America meets *The Bell Curve*'s criteria for a place where "the stuff of community life had to be carried out by the neighborhood or it wouldn't get done," a time when "society was full of accessible valued places for people of a broad range of abilities" (p. 538). For all intents and purposes, federal authority did not exist; "local control" reigned supreme, and a small number of white men were in control of everything.

In fact, of course, the days of Jim Crow were a bit more complicated than Herrnstein and Murray's simple-minded scenario would suggest. Stepping back from their historical idyll, we might note that the authors see the past, like the present, as static, as they blissfully ignore the complex interplay of political and economic factors that have always shaped social structure. In the postbellum South, and in the early twentieth-century North, white tradesmen and skilled workers gradually displaced the few black artisans who plied their trades. This process of course had nothing to do with intelligence and everything to do with the politics of discrimination; white trades unions served as gatekeepers to their crafts, and white craftsmen appealed to "race loyalty" in order to lure customers away from their black competitors. For their part, employers had good reason to discriminate in hiring regardless of the qualifications of workers. For example, black people were excluded from the position of department store clerk because store owners feared that white customers would not patronize their establishments if served by a black man or woman.

In keeping with their wide-eyed, romantic view of the past, Herrnstein and Murray often get their facts wrong when they make tentative forays into the thicket of historical specificity. They refer to "the urbanizing process following slavery" (328), ignoring the half century when the vast majority of former slaves and their children lived in the rural South, and toiled as sharecroppers, before the Great Migration beginning in 1916. The authors also assert that "the wealthy people have always been the most mobile" (p. 104), when in fact sharecroppers had extraordinarily high rates of residential mobility; every year or two, desperately poor families sought out a better deal, a better contract, down the road—or they were evicted by landlords who hoped to find more compliant tenants. The statement that "poverty among children has always been much higher in families headed by a single woman, whether she is divorced or never married" (p. 137) has little relevance to the history of sharecroppers; though they were among the poorest people in the nation, they by and large lived in two-parent households, and those rates of familial stability were the same for black as well as white families. And finally, the authors of *The Bell Curve* write that "as late as the 1940s, so many people were poor in economic terms that to be poor did not necessarily mean to be distinguishable from the rest of the population in any other way" (p. 129). The fact that the poor had less money than the rich "was almost the only reliable difference between the two groups" (p. 129). No doubt sharecrop-

pers of both races would have taken comfort from the idea that
their lives in the cotton fields, and outside the burgeoning consumer
economy, were really not all that different from those of middle-
class urban dwellers at the same time.

The Bell Curve proceeds, or rather, recedes, from Jim Crow back
to the slave South. In order to refute the idea that a legacy of slavery has affected the IQ of African Americans in a negative way, the
authors suggest that Africans as a group are "very dull"; they cite a
researcher who reports "median black African IQ to be 75,
approximately 1.7 standard deviations below the U.S. overall population average, about ten points lower than the current figure for
American blacks" (p. 289). These data suggest to Herrnstein and
Murray that (as they delicately put it) "the special circumstances of
American blacks" (p. 289) have not depressed the group's IQ
scores at all. Indeed, we might assume that the authors mean to
suggest just the opposite—that slavery was a school of sorts, an
institution that helped mentally deficient Africans adapt to a superior way of living.

Many large slave-owning planters, as well as their early twentieth-century scholarly apologists, would have agreed with this assessment. In 1856 the planter-politician William J. Grayson of South
Carolina waxed poetic about the benefits of slavery as an educational institution, and about the pedagogical skills of slave owners:
"Taught by the master's efforts, by his care/ Fed, clothed, protected
many a patient year,. . . / The negroes schooled by slavery embrace/
The highest portion of the Negro race." Samuel Cartwright, a New
Orleans physician, agreed that the slave plantation was "gradually
and silently converting the African barbarian into a moral, rational,
and civilized being."

On the plantation, blacks and whites coexisted in a relatively
peaceful way (though the peace was enforced with violence or the
threat of it). Since black people often made (and make) bad parents—as *The Bell Curve* puts it—a planter no doubt felt justified in
exercising paternalistic control over his workers, sending mothers
and fathers to the field each day while an elderly slave woman
minded their children; or perhaps he felt that it was in his best interest, and the interest of "society in general" if the children were sep-

arated from their parents and sold to another owner. Because the slave family had no legal standing, by definition all slave children were illegitimate; hence their parents hardly deserved to have much control over them in any case. Herrnstein and Murray argue that people with low IQs lack the personal qualities necessary for citizenship because they are not "civilized." They also suggest that today, dumb people commit more crimes than their smart counterparts; we might conclude, then, that the system of slavery was meant to control "uncivilized" people, since "civilized' people do not need to be tightly constrained by laws or closely monitored by organs of the state" (p. 254). As a social institution mediating between the rigors of a complex society and the low-IQ people who lived in it (nineteenth-century America inhabited by the descendants of low-IQ Africans), slavery was superior to any school. In any case, the slave plantation operated on the principle that all low-IQ persons (i.e., blacks) could work productively and should be taken care of accordingly—a virtue in any society (p. 547). If we extrapolate from Herrnstein and Murray's analysis—and understand the planter as a paternalistic smart white man overseeing lots of hardworking black males and fecund "wenches," and controlling the "Nats" predisposed to violent crime or rebellion—then the slave plantation takes on a more benevolent, or at least socially useful, cast.

Antebellum slavery rested on several ideological foundations—the notions that blacks were inherently (intellectually and otherwise) inferior to whites, that some groups must do the dirty work while others govern, and that inequality of ability—and legal rights—was fundamental to an orderly, stable society. James Henry Hammond, a South Carolina slave owner, articulated the antebellum version of *The Bell Curve.* Hammond argued that all societies "have a natural variety of classes. The most marked of these must, in a country like ours, be the rich and the poor, the educated and the ignorant." Hammond, like Herrnstein and Murray, conflated poor people with those of limited intellectual abilities. And like his late-twentieth century ideological successors, Hammond was convinced that the cognitive underclass had no part to play in government at any level; the beauty of slavery was that it rendered the issues of rights and representation among the poor and ignorant a moot question, since this benighted class was rightly "excluded from all participation in the management of public affairs."

Again, what is striking about *The Bell Curve* is the way it offers some very old ideas in the guise of fresh statistics-based revelations. In their claims of scholarly disinterestedness the authors seem to have taken a page out of one of the weighty tomes written by Josiah Nott, an Alabama physician who was also a slavery apologist. In his book *Types of Mankind*, published in 1854, and other works, Nott argued that blacks were inherently inferior to whites and that statesmen, rather than wasting their time on issues related to "the perfectibility of races," might better "deal, in political argument, with the simple facts as they stand." Those "facts" included the idea that no "full-blooded Negro. . . has ever written a page worthy of being remembered." Nott claimed that he was first and foremost a scientist, and that it was up to others to translate his conclusions into social practice: of the inequality of the races, he noted, "It may be proper to state. . . that the subject shall be treated purely as one of science, and that [researchers like himself] will follow facts wherever they may lead, without regard to imaginary consequences."

Not content to tarry in antebellum Dixie, the authors of *The Bell Curve* continue their march back into time with a final chapter, entitled "A Place for Everyone." Here the wisdom of the Founding Fathers is revealed; these slaveholding men inspire hope for the future not because they invented a rhetoric that has informed some of world's great struggles for human rights, but rather, for the opposite reason: because they "wrote frankly about the inequality of men" (p. 530). Jefferson, for example, according to the authors of *The Bell Curve*, "was thankful for a 'natural aristocracy' that could counterbalance the deficiencies of others, an 'aristocracy of virtue and talent, which Nature has wisely provided for the direction of the interests of society'" (p. 530). The new nation was founded by the cognitive elite, and it is to the social ideal that they represented that the nation must return; "in reminding you of these views of the men who founded America, we are not appealing to their historical eminence, but to their wisdom. We think they were right" (p. 532). The great lesson to be learned from the era of the Revolution was that "the ideology of equality has done some good. . . . But most of its effects are bad" (p. 533).

Herrnstein and Murray neglect to mention that Jefferson himself was one of the first white Americans to test the waters of scientific racism; in this respect his ideas served as a bridge of sorts between the seventeenth-century emphasis on blacks as dangerous people, to the antebellum view that blacks were dumb and immoral. During much of the colonial period, blacks were described as wily, cunning, thievish, and recalcitrant—that is, they were described by privileged whites in the same terms used to describe a variety of other groups of subordinate workers, including Irish servants, imported English convicts, and Indian day workers. As a group, then, Africans and their descendants in this country were not so different from other groups of bound laborers; all of these groups resisted the demands imposed upon them by their masters, and all of them, either singly or collectively, posed threats to civil order. Thomas Jefferson, as one of the leading political theorists of his day, was able to mediate between old doctrines that justified the social control of potentially rowdy workers, and new theories of equality; he did this by arguing that black people were fundamentally different from white people.

Like Herrnstein and Murray, Jefferson was intrigued by "the real differences that nature has made" among different groups of people. Writing in *Notes on the State of Virginia,* first published in 1787, Jefferson suggested that blacks' "existence appears to participate more of sensation than reflection." He felt justified in offering this generalization, even allowing for this group's "difference of condition, of education, of conversation, of the sphere in which they move" (that is, the "special circumstances" of American blacks, noted by Herrnstein and Murray above). Unlike those Southerners who, half a century later, would expand upon his views and offer a full-blown defense of slavery, Jefferson simply recorded his observations: "Comparing them by their faculties of memory, reason, and imagination, it appears to me, that in memory they are equal to the whites, in reason much inferior, as I think one could scarcely be found capable of tracking and comprehending the investigations of Euclid, and that in imagination they are dull, tasteless, and anomalous." Assuming that comprehension of "the investigations of

Euclid" amounted to the eighteenth-century equivalent of an IQ test, it is clear that Jefferson shared with Herrnstein and Murray a contempt for the intellectual abilities of black people, and for their potential as members of the body politic.

The Bell Curve authors thus seem relatively restrained in the praise they heap upon their soulmate, the sage of Monticello. Jefferson's rhetoric about equality would later become appropriated by a number of different groups—by slaves and their abolitionist allies, and by women's rights advocates. Yet within the late-eighteenth century social and political context, Jefferson was very much a man of his time, and his place, the slaveholding state of Virginia. If The Bell Curve is right, he was also, apparently, a man for our own time—postindustrial America.

Herrnstein and Murray suggest that "concepts such as virtue, excellence, beauty and truth should be reintroduced into moral discourse" (p. 534). Along with a literal of rendition the Founding Father's political theory, they might as well endorse the social structure that went with it. This, in essence, they do. Just as Madison, Jefferson, and Washington saw slavery as the best way to contain a potentially violent group of poor people—contain them and at the same time confine them to the lowliest kinds of work—so do The Bell Curve authors seek to contain the modern "underclass." Americans are "already afraid of the underclass," and, in the coming years they are "going to have a lot more to be afraid of" (p. 518).

The Bell Curve calls for a devolution of America into a more simple time and place, one where the federal government has receded so that a *wide range of social functions. . . [can] be restored to the neighborhood when possible and otherwise to the municipality*" (p. 540). The anti-Federalists would feel vindicated; but time was not on their side. Late eighteenth-century Republicanism was predicated on a nation of sturdy, independent yeomen farmers, men deferential to their social betters. By the mid-nineteenth century the ideal of widespread landownership had already slipped out of the reach of many Americans; society was highly stratified, with large numbers of wage hands replacing small family farmers. Likewise, it is difficult to see how today's high-tech economy and global assembly line might be compressed to fit into the villages and plantations of late-eighteenth century rural America.

It is worth noting that, throughout the authors' stroll down the backroads and byways of America's past, women remain conspicuous for their absence, except as they make brief, unwanted appearances as the media of murder and mayhem—that is, as reproducers of the Cognitive Mudsill. Here Herrnstein and Murray boldly depart from the Founding Fathers' appreciation of the fact that slave women of child-bearing age were just as valuable as the strongest male field hands. Postindustrial America has no need for more dumb babies, and the authors make it clear that the federal government should stop subsidizing this kind of sociopathological activity. Gone are the days when a bumper tobacco or cotton crop could siphon off the potentially destructive energies of low-IQ people of all ages.

Still, in a book devoted to heritable differences between groups, it is strange to find so little discussion of gender. For example, we might expect the authors to take note of the fact that men seem to do better on math tests than women, and run with it—straight to some straight-faced pronouncements about the inability of women to live in an increasingly complex world. However, the sexual division of labor presents *The Bell Curve* authors with some problems that they prefer not to deal with. During the three historical periods discussed above, women remained disenfranchised and relegated to the margins of the body politic by discriminatory property laws and other forms of state-sanctioned bias. They performed gender-specific work inside and outside the home, much of it unwaged in any case. If, as the authors suggest, "the job market has been rewarding not just formal education but also intelligence" (p. 96), how do we account for the fact that the vast majority of women today inhabit the "pink collar ghetto" of the labor force? If men and women are equal in IQ (see the nine lines devoted to this topic on page 275), and if women are reaching parity with men in terms of college education, it is clear that mediating factors must be keeping women from achieving their due in terms of jobs. My hunch is that, for Herrnstein and Murray to acknowledge that a whole host of political and economic imperatives, as well as individual choices, keep women out of the jobs for which their IQs might qualify them, the two authors might have to depart from their monocausal theory of social structure.

The Bell Curve furthers the currently fashionable agenda of demonizing poor women of both races. Indeed, the authors provide much fodder for the notion that unwed mothers are the root cause of everything that plagues this nation. These women, charge the authors, indulge themselves by living off the goodwill of long-suffering taxpayers. They produce low-birth weight babies with low IQs, babies who will themselves grow up to become chronic welfare recipients and abusive parents—and if they are boys, violent criminals, and if they are girls, irresponsible citizens and the mothers of even more living social time bombs.

The Bell Curve focuses its ire on poor women; the authors suggest for example that "going on welfare really is a dumb idea, and that is why women who are low in cognitive ability end up there" (p. 201). Yet for all of their discussions of jobs and opportunity and civic responsibility, the authors shy away from confronting the political implications of the nation's largest group of dependent (shall we call them selfish and parasitical?) people—the middle-class wives and mothers who stay home full time with their children. Why are poor women who want to attend to their children a threat to the Republic, while middle-class women who do the same thing are heralded as guardians of the nation's "family values"? Why is it so important that welfare mothers betake themselves to the nearest employment office, while middle-class women who choose to work are decried as the embodiment of all neuroses? For all of their self-proclaimed intellectual derring-do, Herrnstein and Murray avoid these issues; instead, they favor glib generalizations that will no doubt prove fodder for any number of right-wing demagogues.

Herrnstein and Murray must deny history, and replace it with mythology, in order to justify a social structure that will keep black people disproportionately relegated to the jobs of nursing aides, orderlies and attendants, cleaners and servants, maids and horsemen. In *The Bell Curve* they suggest that the great threat to American society today is not radical socioeconomic inequality *per se,* but rather all of the loud and rude complaints that emanate from those who are resentful of this inequality. Though they coyly refrain from endorsing a "custodial state" ("we have in mind a high-tech and more lavish version of the Indian reservation for a substantial minority of the nation's population" [p. 526]), the authors put their implicit stamp of approval on policies that at least point in that direction. For example, they propose that the city of Washington, D.C., reject affirmative action and return "to a policy of hiring the best-qualified candidates" for its police department, a policy that will inevitably mean that "a smaller proportion of those new police would be black." Then, they add, "the quality of the Washington police force is likely to improve, which will be of tangible benefit to the hundreds of thousands of blacks who live in that city" (p. 507). Here is the distilled essence of *The Bell Curve*: a call for a city composed largely of black workers to be controlled by white police officers. The notion that white cops will perform their jobs well by virtue of their relatively high IQs is absurd on the face of it; but more significantly, this vision of the well-ordered city exists outside the realm of history, and thus outside the realm of reason. As an artifact of the late twentieth century, then, *The Bell Curve* amounts to hate literature with footnotes.

Why Now?

HENRY LOUIS GATES, JR.

Writing in 1854, Frederick Douglass observed that "pride and self-ishness, combined with mental power, never want for a theory to justify them—and when men oppress their fellow-men, the oppressor ever finds, in the character of the oppressed, a full justification for his oppression. Ignorance and depravity, and the inability to rise from degradation to civilization and respectability, are the most usual allegations against the oppressed. The evils most fostered by slavery and oppression are precisely those which slaveholders and oppressors would transfer from their system to the inherent character of their victims. Thus the very crimes of slavery become slavery's best defense. By making the enslaved a character fit only for slavery, they excuse themselves for refusing to make the slave a free man. A wholesale method of accomplishing this result is to overthrow the instinctive consciousness of the common brotherhood of man. For let it be once granted that the human race are multitudinous origin, naturally different in their moral, physical, and intellectual capacities, and at once you make a plausible demand for classes, grades and conditions, for different methods of culture, different moral, political, and religious institutions, and a chance is left for slavery, as a necessary institution."

The work of Murray and Herrnstein, on the supposedly natural or genetic causes of the discrepancy between black and white Americans on standardized IQ tests, it seems to me, conforms uncannily to Frederick Douglass's fears.

Many of us remember similar conclusions argued for by Arthur J. Jensen and William Shockley in the late 1960s and early 1970s. I

recall a brilliant lecture, critiquing Jensen's work, delivered by my
biology professor at Yale, Arthur Galston, about Jensen's stubborn
refusal to account for the complex interplay between environment
and genetics, and the flaws in his work resulting from this refusal.
In our discussion section, directed by a graduate student named
Donna Harraway, we discussed the public policy implications of
Jensen's work in a Nixon-Agnew administration hell-bent on over-
turning compensatory education programs (such as Head Start),
which had by 1969 become such a fundamental part of what
remained of Lyndon Johnson's War on Poverty.

So what's new, this time around? What's new is that Murray and
Herrnstein's thesis is introduced into public policy deliberations a
quarter of a century after we listened to Galston's refutation, a
quarter of a century that has witnessed the creation of the largest
black middle class in history, as well as the largest black underclass.
Precisely because of those governmental programs that aimed to
ameliorate the environmental causes of poverty, the black middle
class has quadrupled since 1967. Simultaneously, however, almost
45 percent of all black children live at or beneath the poverty line.
Just as the gap between the composite white and black communities
has widened, according to Andrew Hacker, into "two nations," so
too has the gap *within* the black community, between the middle
and working classes on the one hand, and the underclass on the
other.

It is not surprising, therefore, that Murray and Herrnstein's thesis emerges at *this* point in our history—a point at which emphasis
on the *behavioral* causes of poverty are increasingly called upon to
account for the repeating structures of black impoverishment, and
second, when the costs of expanding the size of the black middle
class would seem to have dampened the enthusiasm of liberals in
Congress for the equivalent of a Marshall Plan for our cities, a commitment of our resources sufficient to shift the black bell curve of
class so that it conforms to that of the society as a whole. If differences of intelligence and, therefore, attainment, are *natural*, are
genetic, are ordained by God, then why bother? It won't matter
anyway. And this, it seems to me, is the most pernicious aspect of
Murray and Herrnstein's dismissal of the role of environment in the

performance of blacks on standardized tests: that the gap between *black* haves and have-nots is a reflection of natural variations within the group, and is not a function of the cutbacks in the very federal programs that helped to create the new black middle class in the first place. As Frederick Douglass might say, "The crimes of discrimination have become discrimination's best defense."

Caste, Crime, and Precocity

ANDREW HACKER

Richard Herrnstein and Charles Murray have written a book that deserves reflection and respect. The hallmark of a serious study is not simply that it rouses its readers to argue, but that it compels them to review their own assumptions. *The Bell Curve* has had this effect on me, as few other works have. Of course, as the coming pages will make clear, I reject many of its findings and most of its conclusions. But the book has made me think why I hold the views I do. While I may seem to cast Herrnstein and Murray as adversaries, I esteem them as equals in this arena of ideas.

PHILOSOPHERS AND PORTERS

It will save time if I aver my full agreement with Howard Gardner, who reminds us that there are many kinds of intelligences. (*The Bell Curve* never explores the nuances of Gardner's position.) Indeed, there are many skills and aptitudes that do not even get this designation. We hardly ever speak of an "intelligent poet" or an "intelligent sculptor" or, for that matter, an "intelligent chef." Nor do we often hear someone described as an "intelligent lover." Nor am I sure that we perceive a bootstrap entrepreneur as being an "intelligent businessman." (Some polished corporate types may win that appellation.) These and other talents tend to be regarded as intuitive traits, perhaps having their sources in the torso rather than the cerebrum.

Indeed, what is usually thought of as "intelligence" is more an academic concern than in the working world. To continue with an example just cited, men and women who have proved themselves in

business are often suspicious of people who own more than one
degree. This is why Adam Smith, the philosopher of a free economy, was an egalitarian in the matter of mental endowments. The
people he saw building enterprises had seldom done well on school-
masters' tests. In his view, even savants like himself were essentially
like other people, save for a verbal veneer. Hence this passage in
Wealth of Nations:

> The difference of natural talents in different men is, in reality,
> much less than we are aware of. . . . The difference between the
> most dissimilar characters, between a philosopher and a street
> porter, for example, seems to arise not so much from nature, as
> from habit, custom, and education.

Some people will show themselves to be adept at one kind of
endeavor, while others excel in other areas. Smith's philosopher
might be agile with abstractions, while his porter knows the ways of
the streets. The former does not possess a better mind, but profits
from the premise that verbal virtuosity bespeaks superior intelligence.

MERITOCRACY OR TESTOCRACY?

The principal source for *The Bell Curve*'s findings and conclusions
is the National Longitudinal Survey of Youth, which has tracked a
sample of Americans from the time they left high school through
their middle thirties. As part of the project, its participants were
given a series of questions taken from the Armed Forces Qualification Test. This examination, given to potential recruits, is generally
geared to high school graduates who do not intend to attend college. Their scores on this test were recomputed to show each person's IQ. Two typical questions appear in the accompanying chart.
   Most readers of this book will probably regard these as easily
answered, calling on average high school skills. Still, almost everyone who has taken the SAT will recall that moment of terror when
faced with 150 such questions, all of them to be answered in the
next 180 minutes. What do these tests test? There is, of course, the
issue of whether even supposedly simple questions can be culturally
biased or favor a certain social stratum. Just to cite a single instance,

----

From a building designer's standpoint, three things that make a
home livable are the client, the building site, and the amount of
money the client has to spend. According to this statement, to
make a home livable:

A. the prospective piece of land makes little difference
B. it can be built on any piece of land
C. the design must fit the owner's income and site
D. the design must fit the designer's income

It costs $0.50 per square yard to waterproof canvas What will it
cost to waterproof a canvas truck cover that is 15' x 24'?

A. $ 6.67
B. $ 18.00
C. $ 20.00
D. $180.00

----

while the word "site" is hardly arcane, it is not one would expect in
a typical teenager's vocabulary. At best, it rewards a prior familiarity
with building construction and real estate. While the aim may be to
measure inborn aptitudes, all tests call for substantive amounts of
acquired knowledge.

Moreover, high scores have a strong correlation with whether
individuals were raised in a setting which habituated them to the
kinds of mental processes the tests assess. I trust that all of us will
grant that a person straight off the streets, no matter how innately
clever, could not answer these questions correctly. However, not
knowing "site" is only part of the story. The very format of the test
determines who will do well. Given that one must produce the
answers at just about a one-a-minute rate, doing well demands that
you have a matrix in your mind that mirrors the multiple-choice
format. In part, this can be assisted through schooling. But some
people also seem to possess an instinctive capacity for unsnarling
these kinds of questions, indeed getting their gist in the first twenty
seconds. This said, we can grant that what is being tested are cer-

tain modes of mental functioning. And what is being rated is the degree to which an individual has this one kind of intelligence.

Those who score well readily gain admission to colleges like Amherst and Stanford, from which they move on to Yale Law School and fellowships at Rockefeller University. These institutions require and reward this bookish form of intelligence, one better suited to seminar problem-solving rather than the rough-and-tumble of an unruly world. So I do not accept Murray and Herrnstein's forecast that a caste of high scorers will come to predominate in positions of power. On the whole, most such persons will peak during their academic years, or perhaps during an initial job they receive on the strength of test results. However, after that they will soon be surpassed by individuals who possess more applied forms of intelligence that are not revealed by tests taken while sitting at desks. People like George Patton, Lee Iacocca, and Newt Gingrich come to mind.

At best, *The Bell Curve* authors have identified not a generic meritocracy, but what could be called a testocracy: individuals possessed of a specialized skill which, on further examination, has little relation or relevance to most human endeavors.

It may well be that Harvard students tend to marry one another—I will have to check the marriage columns—and produce progeny sharing their genes. Yet here, too, I see no caste coming. For one thing, offspring generally regress towards the mean. Let us suppose that one hundred of these Harvard couples each have two children. All of those two hundred scions would have to display Harvard scores if they are to carry on the caste started by their two hundred parents. Yet it seems safe to surmise that upwards of half of these children will have aptitudes other than the sort sought by Harvard admissions officers. Indeed, it is widely known that this august institution finds itself impelled to admit alumni offspring with lesser credentials than other applicants. Not the least cause for this indulgence—a form of affirmative action—is that Harvard parents attain a sufficiently comfortable mode of life, so that their children feel no urgency to overexert themselves. Thus regression to the mean is hastened by a softening brought on by an easy upbringing.

NEGLECTING THE "GIFTED"

For too long, the authors tell us, public funds have been squandered on remedial programs, directed toward youngsters whose deficiencies are really hereditary and hence impervious to remedy. If we are to allocate money, they counsel, it would be better spent on "gifted" children, whose needs have too long been neglected.

As it happens, we hear a great deal about youngsters who have superior minds, largely through the testimony of their parents. Even at early ages, we are told, these children complain of being bored, since they master school assignments well ahead of their classmates. Even worse, we are warned, if there is no recognition of their special gifts, they may give up and end up absorbed by the mediocre many. Hence the calls for segregated sections or streams or even entire schools, so this group will realize its full potential. In these intellectually depressed times, we need all the geniuses we can get.

Here, too, I must demur. We are being asked to show concern for children who are, very simply, precocious. For a variety of reasons, they can cope with school subjects easily and earlier. Some are also quite verbal, and sound like miniature adults. In fact, many of their classmates catch up, and proceed to pass them. We have no evidence that children who read Shakespeare at three, or understand calculus at six, go on to contribute more than others to the intellectual life of the commonweal. I can also attest that undergraduates I have known, who were widely regarded as "brilliant," almost all ended up with quite average careers.

However, I do have a proposal. Isolating and insulating the "gifted" fosters an erroneous estimate of their talents. Instead, let us retain these children in regular classrooms, but give them a special charge. It will be their job to sit with small groups of their agemates, or even one-on-one, and explain the assignments to their putatively "duller" peers. This is what used to happen in one-room schools, where eighth graders helped to teach those just starting. It is one thing to understand the material yourself. But a much more revealing test is whether you can transmit this comprehension to others. Indeed, the ability to explain is just as crucial as a capacity to absorb. On which note, I might suggest that many of our current discontents owe to our lack of attention to this underappreciated art.

HIGH IQ CRIMINALITY

Criminal behavior, *The Bell Curve* reports, is more likely among citizens who are obliged to get by with lesser cognitive capacities. This statement is probably true; or it is so long as it is added that we are referring only to those offenses commonly construed as "street crimes." By these we generally mean stealing vehicles, breaking into private property, or demanding cash or valuables in threatening encounters. Also in the "street" category are violent felonies like rape and murder and aggravated assault. There is no need to underscore the fear the rest of us have of falling victim to these kinds of crimes, and the desire to do whatever can be done to deter that eventuality.

It should not surprise us that people who hold up shops or accost citizens on the streets are unlikely to score well on tests. After all, the reason they commit their crimes outdoors is that they do not have occupations which offer opportunities for less intimidating offenses. (At this point, I am speaking of persons with larcenous proclivities, a relatively small portion of the population but one with members at all social levels.) This said, one might ask why the authors of *The Bell Curve* did not analyze felonious activity that calls for a high intelligence quotient.

While we all know there are other kinds of crimes, they are less in the public mind. One reason is that indoor offenses are less visible. It is not easy to see billions looted from savings and loan associations, or agreements to fix prices or pad costs on public contracts. Nor do we apply the term "violent" to financiers who lure citizens into bogus investments, or physicians who defraud Medicare and Medicaid. Nor is our penchant to fill up prisons aimed at answering the Internal Revenue Service's plaint that persons who conceal income and otherwise evade taxes cost the rest of us at least $150 billion each year. Even so, we are told, in the *Corporate Crime Reporter,* that "white collar and corporate crime injures society far more than all street crimes combined." If these offenses are not seen as threatening, perhaps it is because their commission calls for brains rather than brawn.

Within a single month, the *Corporate Crime Reporter* cited offenses by executives within the following firms: Dow Corning, Sylvania Electric, Metropolitan Life, Exxon, Prudential Securities, Tyson Foods, Continental Airlines, Deloitte & Touche, plus price collusion between the makers of Brillo and SOS soap pads. What emerges in the reports is the high level of mental ability needed to perpetrate corporate crimes, ranging from verbal versatility to mathematical sophistication. It strikes me as anomalous that a book so dedicated to intelligence refrains from mentioning this fertile field for superior minds.

WHY ARE SOME WHITES SMARTER?

I have no problem accepting *The Bell Curve*'s finding that Americans with European forebearers average better on IQ tests than citizens with African ancestries. And for present purposes, I will concede the author's claim that the capacity for scoring well via the multiple-choice method is "substantially heritable."

Yet Herrnstein and Murray also warn that while individuals get their genes through their parents, this inheritance does not entitle us to make race-based generalizations. "That a trait is genetically transmitted in individuals," they write, "does not mean that group differences in that trait are also genetic in origin."

Really? Surely what we know about gene pools suggests that when identifiable groups of human beings live and procreate with one another for considerable periods, certain traits will come to predominate and be reproduced. For a long time, and even now, people we call Koreans have been more likely than not to mate with one another. If this process passes on pigmentation and physical features, why not also the quality and contours of their cognitive capacities?

My aim here will be quite modest. It is to carry Herrnstein and Murray's premise a step further, by applying it to the persons who make up the race they call "white." What I found curious about their analysis is that they treat this extremely large catchment— more than 200 million people according to the last Census—as a singular genetic group. Yet it would seem self-evident that so capacious a conglomerate will contain vital variations. Much more might have been learned had they divided the white population into several sub-races—perhaps by pigmentation or physiognomy—then surveyed the average intelligence of these cohorts.

Of course, the authors might reply that such information is not available. Nor is this surprising. For the last half-century, this country has had an unstated understanding that it not draw genetic distinctions among Americans who have been allowed to identify themselves as white. Religious differences are obviously acknowledged, as are those of national origin. Even so, regardless of whether their forebears came from Stockholm or Sofia or Salerno, all whites are presumed to belong to single gene pool and thus have equal status in the Caucasian category. And while we also take note of social disparities, even the lowest classes of whites are not given a diminished designation. (Epithets like "redneck" and "white trash," once commonly heard, have all but disappeared.) This decision of whites to stand together colors the race-based analysis in *The Bell Curve.**

This was not always the case. Earlier in the century, such social scientists as Henry Goddard and Carl Brigham saw nothing untoward in identifying regional races within Europe which had varying mental capacities. Thus they felt free to pronounce the intellectual primacy of persons of "Nordic" stock, while citing the stunted facilities of swarthier "Mediterranean" and "Alpine" strains. And to sequester the best, they opposed intermarriage. That they rated African Americans even lower goes without saying, as does the happenstance that both of these scholars fell into the Nordic category. Addressing a related concern, they pointed to white families like the "Jukes" and "Kallikaks," as a warning that inbreeding could ravage even Caucasians.

---

*In a similar vein, Hugh Pearson has wondered why no attempt was made to discover whether lighter blacks register higher IQs. Such a study would not be difficult. One could compare the scores of a pool of people resembling Harry Belafonte and Colin Powell with a group more similar to Sidney Poitier and Clarence Thomas.

Due to lack of studies based on smaller gene pools, I have had to avail myself of an alternative measure. The Census provides quite reliable information on the number of persons who have entered and completed college. The following figures refer to the proportion of Americans of various European ancestries who have received bachelors' degrees.

NATURE OR CULTURE?

PROPORTIONS OF AMERICANS WHO HAVE COMPLETED COLLEGE
BY SELF-IDENTIFIED ANCESTRIES

French-Canadian	16.7%
Dutch	18.5%
Italian	21.0%
Irish	21.2%
German	22.0%
Finnish	24.2%
Norwegian	26.0%
Danish	27.4%
Swedish	27.4%
Scotch-Irish	28.2%
English	28.4%
Welsh	31.8%
Scottish	33.6%
Russian	49.0%

Even granting that some groups arrived here earlier, all of those on the list are at least third-generation, which should be sufficient time for their members to enter the college cohort. We can also agree that ambition and discipline, as well as family encouragement, figure in getting to and through college. Still, some mental capacity is needed to achieve a degree; and here Herrnstein and Murray tell us that favorable heredity should not be discounted. Moreover, strong links persist between additional years of schooling and scores on standardized tests. So if more people from a group finish college, that attainment will raise its average IQ.

If genetic causes can be evoked to explain mental differences between blacks and whites, then we might search for similar sources within the white group. Persons of Russian ancestry, who happen to be predominantly Jewish and hence of "Mediterranean" origin, spent much of their evolution well apart from the "Nordic" Dutch. While cultural factors obviously play a role, might not something within white gene pools lead to disparate representation in higher education? I don't know. What I find revealing, though, is that no one seems inclined to find it.

Of course, we know the reason. Undertaking such studies could pit whites against whites, which would be politically imprudent. Better, then, to focus on presumed black deficiencies, a tactic which is neither surprising nor new.

"EACH IN THEIR APPOINTED PLACE"

In the tradition of serious thought, Richard Herrnstein and Charles Murray have a vision of a better society. In their closing pages, they urge us to create a world in which all human beings can achieve their fullest potential. Such an aim need not be utopian, but a reasonable ideal which even imperfect creatures may aspire to attain. Adam Smith's market competition was one such model; so is the United Nations design for collective for security.

The Bell Curve would have us move towards an order in which all citizens understand their intellectual limitations, and accede to places consonant with those abilities. Too many of our current practices, we are told, subvert this precept. Thus the problem with affirmative action in education and employment is that it propels people into tiers beyond their capacities. Not only does society suffer from incompetence in high places, but individuals so elevated become frustrated and defensive.

While the authors never say so directly, one senses that they would like to inform everyone of their intelligence quotients at an early age, so they can choose careers within their mental ambit. This would call for careful counseling, with caveats to parents not to push their offspring in inappropriate directions. As it happens, this position has ancient antecedents, beginning well before the advent of scientific testing. It was stated best by Edmund Burke, building on the assumptions of Socrates and Plato. "The legislators who framed the ancient republics," Burke wrote, "thought themselves obliged to dispose their citizens into such classes, and to place them in such situations in the state, as their peculiar habits might qualify them to fill." To do this, he continued, would simply reflect the natural order of the world:

> Each contract of each particular state is but a clause in the great primeval contract of eternal society, linking the lower with the higher natures, connecting the visible and invisible world, according to a fixed compact sanctioned by the inviolable oath which holds all physical and all moral natures, each in their appointed place.

If all of us can be led to accept our "appointed place," the result will be personal happiness and social stability. Those of high ability and deserved responsibilities will be able to find cheerful and deferential servitors to mow their lawns and clean their homes. We will also have a class of skilled and reliable artisans, who take pride in their callings. In addition, they will charge appropriate fees, realizing what is their rightful due. And if governance follows the Burkean model, citizens will grant that rule belongs to those best able to conduct matters of state. In return, all will be honored and respected for jobs well done, without condescension on one side or envy on the other.

To which must be added a further *Bell Curve* corollary: if members of some races are found, on average, to be less suited for larger responsibilities, they should accept this as nature's dictate and not human artifice.

REFERENCES

Ancestry of the Population in the United States, Bureau of the Census (August 1993), Tables 3, 5.

Armed Services Vocational Aptitude Battery: Student and Parent Guide, Department of Defense (July 1992), pp. 16, 18.

Burke, Edmund, *Reflections on the Revolution in France* (London: Dent, 1910), 94, 180.

Corporate Crime Reporter (Washington, D.C.: American Communications and Publishing, November 1993).

Gardner, Howard, *Frames of Mind: The Theory of Multiple Intelligences* (New York: Basic Books, 1983).

Goleman, Daniel, "Successful Executives Rely on Own Kind of Intelligence," *New York Times* (July 31, 1984), C1.

Pearson, Hugh, "Race Matters," *The New Republic* (October 31, 1994), 16.

Smith, Adam, *The Wealth of Nations* (New York: Modern Library, 1937), 7.

Has There Been a Cognitive Revolution in America? The Flawed Sociology of The Bell Curve

ALAN WOLFE

I

The publication of *The Bell Curve* has launched a furious debate about race, genetics, and intelligence. Yet a good deal of what Richard Herrnstein and Charles Murray have to say about those highly contentious subjects rests on a prior point, which I want to make the focus of this commentary.

The book argues that what is taking place in America is an unprecedented revolution, perhaps the most momentous event in world history. In a statement as sweeping as one can imagine, Herrnstein and Murray write that "from the beginning of history into this century," cognitive screening existed without the existence of a cognitive elite. But in the late twentieth century, a new elite emerged, based neither on hereditary advantage nor on place in the means of production, but on brains. Overclass and underclass are divided by cognition; the smart will rule and the dumb will follow. The implications of this are ominous: "The fragile web of civility, mutual regard, and mutual obligations at the heart of any happy society begins to tear." *The Bell Curve* is a *Communist Manifesto* for the mind—a stirring, but portentous, announcement of a new world order recently come into being.

A moment's reflection should indicate why the theory of the cognitive elite, though less overtly controversial than questions of race and genetics, is the crucial linchpin in Herrnstein's and Murray's argument. A society can be cognitively unequal and yet socially just—the extremely bright, overcome with neurosis, can fail in life, while the less than brilliant, through dint of common sense, can succeed. Democracy attaches far less importance to intelligence than to moderation, virtue, loyalty, hard work, obedience, fairness, and respect. Differences between classes, races, and genders with respect to intelligence, if they exist, are far less divisive if abilities other than cognition determine life chances, for there would be many paths to success, each with its own importance. A just society, as Michael Walzer has observed, is one that contains many spheres, each with its own criteria of distributive justice, so long as one does not dominate all the rest.

But if one sphere does dominate the rest, advantages become transferable, leading to the perpetuation of differences. Herrnstein and Murray argue that intelligence is becoming such a dominant sphere. If they are right, one must be concerned with the distribution of intelligence between groups and the persistence of such distributive patterns over time. For if intelligence is not only going to determine today's ruling elite, but all future ruling elites as well, how could one *not* address how intelligence is passed from one generation to another? The theory of the cognitive elite makes the discussion of genetics and racial differences plausible; take away the theory of the cognitive elite, and *The Bell Curve* would be roughly like Christopher Jenck's *Equality*—controversial, worthy of debate, informative, but hardly the stuff of invective and accusations of bad faith.

Is, then, the theory of the cognitive elite true? One tiny part of it surely is, for there can be little doubt that American society became somewhat more meritocratic in recent years (with merit understood as intellectual ability). Herrnstein and Murray begin their book by pointing out that the average student admitted to Harvard in 1952 would have been in the bottom of the class admitted in 1960, so great was the increase in standards during that eight-year period.

Yet that very point also illustrates something even more important about intelligence in America, one unremarked by Herrnstein and Murray. It is surprising how late the notion of a meritocracy came to American life; the 1960s, the age of the unlamented "best and the brightest," was the first time in American history where the possession of intelligence seemed to be something about which one actually bragged. And, one hastens to add, intelligence did not do so well; the war in Vietnam and failed domestic initiatives are often attributed to the overweening arrogance of the smart.

No wonder, then, that intelligence, which arrived late, departed early. By the 1980s, Ronald Reagan's genial populism had deflated brains on the right, while affirmative action had dealt merit a death blow on the left. The fact is that neither the right nor the left likes brightness. Conservatives would rather base the affairs of state on breeding (in Britain) or sympathy for the "forgotten man" (in America). Radicals do not like brains either; although using intelligence to divide people into ranks may be among the fairer ways of making distinctions, they are distinctions nonetheless and unacceptable to those who reject any difference, let alone hierarchical ones.

For a cognitive elite to emerge in America, in short, it would have to do so against the grain of American culture, which has been anti-intellectual and populistically democratic. Such a revolution could still have happened; culture, after all, can change. But culture changes so slowly that it is highly unlikely that any events of the past twenty or thirty years, even more meritocratic admissions standards at elite universities and professional schools, could barely dent it. We are not France. Rather than recruit our business and governmental elites based on national examinations, we try to find ways to cut corners on whatever examinations we have so that the economically privileged but not too bright can still do well. The burden of proof lies against the hypothesis that a cognitive revolution has taken place in American life. Herrnstein and Murray will have to make a very persuasive case for it if the normative and speculative accounts of their treatise are to be taken seriously.

II

If we forget, for the moment, Plato's philosopher king, the notion of a cognitive elite originated in the ideas of Henri, Comte de Saint-Simon, who, in 1803, warned the "conservative property owners of France" that they were going to be pushed to the limits by "scholars and artists." It has been a popular idea ever since; one can find expressions of the notion in writers as varied as William James, Thorstein Veblen, James Burnham, Adolf Berle, Milovan Djilas, George Konrad, Peter Drucker, and Pierre Bourdieu. Intellectuals obviously like the idea of rule by intelligence, so much so that they have been predicting its emergence for close to two hundred years.

A recent version of the story of a cognitive elite, called the theory of the new class, emerged from every point on the political spectrum in the 1970s. On the left, Barbara and John Ehrenreich pondered the existence of a "professional and managerial class," one that, existing halfway between owners and workers, nonetheless seemed to them to side with the forces of the status quo. In the center, Daniel Bell argued for the emergence of a postindustrial society, a new "axis" in which knowledge would become the organizing principle of the division of labor. Conservative writers, trying to understand why the New Left appealed more to upper-middle-class graduate students than manual workers, turned the theory of the new class on its head. From their point of view, intellectuals, having imbibed Lionel Trilling's "adversary culture," were not a new ruling class but a new revolutionary class. The push for everything from socialist revolution to government regulation was being led, they argued, by university-trained radicals who were seriously out of touch with the "old classes," both bourgeois *and* proletariat.

The theory of the new class never really took hold. Postindustrial society did emerge, but it hardly displaced industrial society; caught between international competition and the need for votes from workers, governments tried to protect industry as best they could. A communications and information revolution took place, but it did so in industrial form, complete with assembly production, market-driven priorities, and managerial consolidation; *wunderkinder* such as Steve Jobs, whose entrepreneurial success was based on brain power, were forced out in favor of traditional industrial bureaucrats. Nor did the new class triumph in the form of a leftist seizure of power; no sooner had conservatives advanced the idea than the country, and with it a substantial part of the intellectual elite, turned conservative. The theory of the new class was even found not to apply in the Eastern bloc countries where it had had its greatest success, for intellectuals, although important in the revolution against communism, quickly gave way to traditional politicians. Only in France—always the exception—have intellectuals retained their power as a class; "cultural capital," to use Bourdieu's phrase, is as important in France as it always has been.

Despite the failure of the theory of the new class to take hold generally, it survived in one form that would be adopted by Herrnstein and Murray. Robert Reich, a political economist who would become Secretary of Labor in the Clinton Administration, argued in *The Work of Nations* that a class of "symbol analysts"—devoted to "lifetimes of creative problem-solving, identifying, and brokering"—had emerged in America. This was not, from Reich's perspective, good news. American society was becoming increasingly divided between the symbol analysts and everyone else, he felt. The former congregated in the tonier zip codes, sent their children to private schools, worked long hours, and competed furiously to ensure admission to elite colleges for their offspring. The symbol of the new America, in Reich's view, is the "common interest development," a suburban enclave protected by private police, in which residents assess themselves for services which benefit only themselves, unwilling to pay taxes which might help the less fortunate. Reich concluded that "symbol analysts in effect withdraw their dollars from the support of public spaces shared by all and dedicate the savings to private spaces they share with other symbol analysts."

Reich was not the only writer to advance this version of the theory of the new class. Historian Christopher Lasch has written about "the revolt of the elite," by which he means the disdain shown by the brainy and the talented toward the conventional morality and common sense wisdom of the lower middle class. Lasch is even more negative toward the symbol analysts than Reich. For Lasch, the cognitive elite comes dangerously close to disloyalty; many of the top 20 percent of Americans "have ceased to think of themselves as Americans in any important sense, implicated in America's destiny for better or worse." Not always clear who belongs to this elite—at one point it is George Bush and another it is tenured academics—Lasch, like Herrnstein and Murray, has no doubt that "the new aristocracy of brains" is what matters. Moreover, the cognitive elite is reproducing itself. In *The Bell Curve*, Herrnstein and Murray argue that "the propensity to mate by cognitive ability has increased." Lasch agrees. The same top 20 percent of the population that withdraws its allegiance from America reinforces its privileged position through "assortative mating"—"the tendency of men to marry women who can be relied on to bring in income more or less equivalent to their own."

Herrnstein and Murray believe strongly in the theory of the new class: "Membership in this new class, the cognitive elite, is gained by high IQ; neither social background, nor ethnicity, nor lack of money will bar the way." In contemplating its implications, they cite Reich approvingly. When they discuss *New Yorker* writer Pauline Kael's comment that Richard Nixon could not have won because she did not know anyone who voted for him, they sound very much like Lasch. The following words are from Herrnstein and Murray, but they could just as easily have been written by Reich (or Lasch): "The members of the cognitive elite are likely to have gone to the same kinds of schools, live in similar neighborhoods, go to the same kinds of theaters and restaurants, read the same magazines and newspapers, watch the same television programs, even drive the same makes of cars."

Herrnstein and Murray, in short, have adopted an idea that has surface plausibility and that has been endorsed by some of America's most interesting social critics. But the question remains: Is it true? Neither Reich nor Lasch even tries to make a case that it is; one finds in neither of their books survey data, the analysis of behavioral variables, ethnographic accounts—indeed any actual evidence that the upper middle class has detached itself from the rest of America. When Herrnstein and Murray write that "the isolation of the cognitive elite is by no means complete, but the statistical tendencies are strong," they fail to document any such "statistical tendencies." (They do provide data on cognitive sorting by education and jobs, which I will turn to shortly.) As this lack of evidence suggests, there is good reason to doubt that anything like a cognitive elite has emerged. But the reader need not take my word for this. Some of the best evidence against the conclusion that we have witnessed the emergence of a distinct cognitive elite has been provided by Herrnstein and Murray themselves.

III

Herrnstein and Murray try to establish the existence of a cognitive elite by demonstrating that both educational opportunities and jobs are partitioned by IQ to a much greater degree now than ever before. College must act as a sorting mechanism if the theory of the cognitive elite is to be substantiated. Such sorting should take place on two levels. First, colleges themselves will have to be partitioned; bad students will get into bad colleges, while good students will get into good ones. Second, in both kinds of colleges, but especially in the latter, IQ will sort good students from worse students, so that only the former can obtain and advance in the jobs that require brains. Herrnstein and Murray provide some interesting information on the first point; they demonstrate how different quality colleges do indeed attract differently accomplished students. That, however, merely testifies to the existence of class differences in America and to a relationship between class and SAT scores—hardly news. The more important point is the latter one. To support the theory of the cognitive elite, we need to know whether performance at a top college predicts success later in mentally demanding careers.

Former Harvard president Derek Bok argued that "test scores have a modest correlation with first-year grades and no correlation at all with what you do in the rest of your life." How do Herrnstein and Murray respond? First they admit that Bok is both "poetically" and "technically" correct; in other words, they concede that there is no relationship between test scores in college, even at Harvard, and later career success. The point could not be clearer: college admissions is increasingly sorted by brain power, but such sorting means almost nothing once college is over.

Having lost on that point, Herrnstein and Murray quickly shift the focus; they begin to argue that IQ affects, not career success, but job performance. The linkage between IQ and job performance is made, moreover, not by citing science, but by citing scientists; it is "common agreement by the leading contemporary scholars" that should persuade us, not actual findings. (They make the same point to refute critics of g; all the scientists agree, therefore g must exist.) Yet in the very paragraph following the proclamation of this "common agreement," they write as follows: "Whereas experts in employee selection accept the existence of the relationship between cognitive ability and job performance, they often disagree with each other's numerical conclusions." It is, of course, the numerical conclusions that matter; a correlation of .2 is entirely different than a correlation of .6.

If *The Bell Curve* was written in a spirit of scientific modesty, it would reject the relationship between IQ and job performance, given how little support for it there is. This is conspicuously what Herrnstein and Murray do not do. They prefer to talk about the relationship "qualitatively" rather than "quantitatively," for "a powerful method of statistical analysis that was developing during the 1970s and came of age in the 1980s" rescues the hypothesis. This technique, meta-analysis, tries to find statistical trends by bringing together results from many different studies. Even specific studies that show no correlations at all can, under meta-analysis, be "full of gold," as Herrnstein and Murray claim in this case. In other words, one can take one disputed statistical artifact, called g, and analyze its effect on another statistical artifact—not job performance, but the combined effect of various (and contradictory) studies of job performance. When the one artifact is correlated with the other, a relationship emerges, which Herrnstein and Murray estimate as .4. How significant is that figure? "The temptation is to say, not very," they concede. And here is their final summation: "As we showed before, there will be many exceptions to the predicted productivity with correlations this modest. And indeed it is not very important when an employer needs just a few new employees for low-complexity jobs and is choosing among a small group of job applicants who have small differences in test scores."

So much for the relationship between IQ and job performance with respect to low-level jobs. What about the brainy sector? Is it true, as they write, that "the upper strata of intelligence *are* being sucked into a comparatively few occupations in a way that they did not used to be?" Once again they have little or no confirmatory data. "Experts," they write, "have come to agree that something beyond education, gender, and experience has been at work to increase income disparities in recent times." Is that "something" intelligence? It turns out that they have no idea. Calling this residual the "X" factor, they note that "it could be rooted in diligence, ambition, or sociability." "Or," they continue, "it could be cognitive ability." In any case, "conclusive evidence is hard to come by." They conclude this crucial point simply by making a hypothesis: whatever causes income disparity in the high-paying jobs, intelligence must be one the factors included. No one would disagree with that, but it is a slim reed on which to hang the notion that cognitive ability has ushered in a revolution never before seen in history.

When all is said and done, IQ predicts neither later success in life nor job performance. It does not predict income disparities later in life. Do we know what the future implications are of increased IQ sorting? Herrnstein and Murray write that "we aren't sure." Even the trend to assortative mating, in which smart people only marry smart people, we are told, has "almost certainly increased," the qualifier being necessary because "no quantitative studies tell whether assortative mating by intelligence has been increasingly recently." There is simply no evidence other than bits of anecdotal scraps that cognition is what divides people into classes in America. A more damning critique of the theory of cognitive elites would be hard to find.

Not only is the theory of cognitive differentiation unsupported by Herrnstein and Murray, their interpretative speculations about its implications are also unpersuasive. "What worries us first about the emerging cognitive elite," they write, "is its coalescence into a class that views American society increasingly through a lens of its own." Herrnstein and Murray, political conservatives, accept one of the crucial tenets of Marxism: class location determines one's outlook on life. They seem to believe that because smart people work in the same kinds of jobs and live in the same kinds of enclaves, they will have the same values. Yet this way of thinking about class, as we now know from the failures of Marxism, is sociologically naive.

First, people who have the same class relationship do not necessarily agree with each other. The "elite" enclaves described by writers such as Reich, Lasch, and Herrnstein and Murray are populated by diverse people with very different points of view. University communities such as Chapel Hill have become the most attractive retirement communities in America, mixing liberal academics and retired military officers with relative ease. Berkeley and Brookline have experienced rebellions against their ultraliberal reputations, led by tired old leftists, wealthy entrepreneurs, recent immigrants, and parents of young children—all fed up with tolerance toward the homeless or high schools without intellectual content. The high-powered communities around Harvard and MIT are home to more scientists and engineers than they are to literary critics; after all, the defense industry financed the growth of Route 128 as much as it did the state of California.

It is even the case that the cognitively well-off do not agree on the very feature that makes them well-off: the possession of intelligence. British capitalists, the historian Martin Weiner has pointed out, developed an anticapitalist culture, aping the aristocracy the moment they could free themselves of the business affairs that made them rich. Similarly, no other group in American society leads the attack on credentials and brains as much as those with credentials and brains (just as no other group thinks that brains provides advantages as much as those without advantages). It is at the elite institutions in American society where the privileges of a cognitive elite are most challenged. Joseph Schumpeter, who did so much to inspire the theory of the new class, pointed out how capitalists have an urge for self-destruction. If a cognitive elite were to emerge, it would not be the first class in world history to commit collective suicide.

From every point of view, ranging from actual data to sociological speculation, there is little if any evidence that an economic class structure has been replaced by a cognitive class structure. Intelligence is not randomly distributed throughout American society; the rich and the privileged tend to have more of it, and Herrnstein and Murray are surely correct that an all too frightening proportion of the "underclass" have less of it. But that point, had they made it, would have little dramatic power, since all it does is call attention to facts long known about social class in America. Herrnstein and Murray go way beyond their data, indeed beyond any data, to make unsupported claims about a cognitive revolution that never took place. This tendency to overinterpret ambiguous data about the extent of a cognitive revolution is worrisome, for it seems to confirm those critics who also argue that they overinterpret ambiguous data about the relationship between race, genes, and intelligence.

IV

It might still be possible to forgive the mistakes made by Herrnstein and Murray if those mistakes were the result of excess enthusiasm for a good thing. After all, there is nothing wrong in wishing for a cognitive revolution to take place; while having some doubts about merit, I, for one, believe that it remains the fairest way to distribute the good things in life. Had Herrnstein and Murray simply wished a more meritocratic society to come into being, and out of that wish exaggerated their case, their science could still be criticized, but not necessarily their values. Oddly, however, they are not enthusiasts for the cognitive revolution they claim has come into existence. If anything, their book is a normative attack on the possibility and desirability of a meritocracy.

"Unchecked," they write about the cognitive revolution they (mistakenly) describe, "these trends will lead the United States toward something resembling a caste society, with the underclass mired ever more firmly at the bottom and the cognitive elite ever firmly anchored at the top." Of all the misuses of IQ testing associated with Murray and Herrnstein, the one that bothers me most is this identification of intelligence with caste. IQ testing, despite its original use against Jews and Catholics, became an attack on the privileges of a hereditary elite; the emphasis on sheer mental power would enable talented second generation immigrants to challenge the WASP aristocracy's control over leading American institutions.

Since no one can predict the future, Herrnstein and Murray could conclude that whatever the differences in IQ between ethnic groups today, a continued reliance on intelligence testing is morally justified because it is the best way of ensuring that talented people from all ethnic groups will get a chance to succeed. This is not, however, how they draw up their speculations about the future. Instead they turn to what they call "the ancient concern with place." We can, they believe, construct a morally defensible society "in which every citizen has access to the central satisfactions of life." In this way, the unintelligent need not despair, for it is perfectly possible to take pride in all kinds of things, including those kinds of work that do not require highly developed mental powers.

Yet what is so wrong with the idea that a society should distribute its scarce resources based on merit? Only two alternatives to it have even been tried in America. One, traditional conservativism, would have breeding and connections serve as the basis of privilege; the other, affirmative action, would turn the advantages of birth upside down. One would think that Herrnstein and Murray, as conservatives, would favor the former and condemn the latter. The truth, however, is more complicated. They actually argue for aspects of both.

American conservatives have rarely been traditionalists; they believe too much in the market for that. The market is theoretically organized on anticaste principles; economic man does not practice racial discrimination if it costs more than it benefits. Herrnstein and Murray cannot simultaneously argue for caste and for laissez-faire. Indeed they do not; their preference is for the former, not the latter. "We fear that a new kind of conservatism is becoming the dominant ideology of the affluent—not in the social tradition of an Edmund Burke or in the economic tradition of an Adam Smith but 'conservatism' along Latin American lines, where to be conservative has often meant doing whatever is necessary to preserve the mansions on the hill from the menace in the slums below." If such a conservatism is emerging, it is because it has its advocates, among them, Herrnstein and Murray. *The Bell Curve* returns American conservatism to the pre-Smithian days when the end of a person's life was determined by the beginning of a person's life.

A Smithian sensibility is quite absent from *The Bell Curve*. Laissez-faire applies as much to population questions as it does to economic ones. One could, as some neoclassical economists do, take the point of view that since people make wealth, and since more wealth is good, there is nothing wrong with having more people. Or one can argue that just as we need economic and social planning to curb the economic market, so we need family and population planning to curb the people market. Herrnstein and Murray lie closer to the latter point of view, which, historically, has been associated with the left: Margaret Sanger, a progressive advocate of birth control, was also in favor of trying to reduce the pressures caused by an excess of poor people. They worry about "dysgenesis"—demographic trends that drive the overall level of intelligence downward. Ignoring the so-called Flynn effect, which points out that IQ rises over time, they opt for apocalyptic scenarios: "The stakes are large and. . . continuing to pretend that there's nothing worth thinking about is as reckless as it is foolish." Herrnstein and Murray have more in common with Malthus than Smith. Their conservatism is not the stuff of open competition, at least with respect to the size of population; it is far more the stuff of ecological limits or lifeboat ethics. The only difference between Herrnstein and Murray and population control enthusiasts is that the former never discuss the two most widely available methods of family planning—birth control and abortion.

There is also a strange affinity between the analysis provided in *The Bell Curve* and the defense of affirmative action. Herrnstein and Murray, to be sure, are strong critics of affirmative action; part of their book is devoted to documenting the economic inefficiencies it produces in the form of foregone intelligence. Furthermore, they admirably refrain from introducing race into their book for hundreds of pages, before finally concluding that they cannot help themselves. Yet when they do turn to race, they do so in a way that bears a striking resemblance to their ideological antagonists on the left. Herrnstein and Murray see the world in group terms and must have data on group membership. If, in the anger over affirmative action, all racial classifications were abolished, it would no longer be possible to design congressional districts or college admissions profiles to account for race. But nor would it be possible to measure the relationship between race and IQ. Would Herrnstein and Murray cheer a result in which they could say as much as they wanted about individual differences in IQ, but they could say nothing about group differences? Clearly they would not. Their entire approach demands that race be reified. If the significance of race were declining, they would have to do everything they could to bring it back. No wonder that multiracialism is alien to their perspective. Herrnstein and Murray find a strong relationship between race and IQ, but neither race nor IQ are strong phenomena. A strong relationship between weak variables is a weak relationship.

In addition Herrnstein and Murray, like their antagonists on the left, endorse a kind of Afrocentric multiculturalism. This is foreshadowed in *The Bell Curve* when they write about how everyone, no matter how dumb, nonetheless can find a valued place in a hierarchical society. What is implicit in the book became explicit in the article Charles Murray wrote for *The New Republic* which summarized and expanded upon the themes of the book. Aligning himself with the sillier aspects of Afrocentrism, he talked about "a distinctive black culture" and argued that "differences need not be sources of resentment; in a suitably pluralistic world, they can be sources of celebration." The ideal society envisioned by these writers is anything but a meritocratic one; it is rather one in which Americans are divided by race, count by race, and take pride in racial differences. That is about as far from the individualistic justification of IQ testing—the notion that tests allow the best individuals from any social group to rise to the top—as one can get.

Because it takes on so many issues, and does so in contentious ways, *The Bell Curve* will be debated for some time. I welcome its publication, if for no other reason than because it brings back to life a rich tradition of sociological speculation about such issues as the importance of cognition, the relationship between cognition and class position, and the moral benefits and pitfalls of meritocracy. These are questions that have been around for close to two centuries. One ventures to guess that they will be around for the next two centuries as well. The notion that these questions have answers—that we can conclude with some certainly that a cognitive revolution has taken place which assigns reward and failure by mental ability—is, however, premature. There simply is no convincing evidence that brains have supplanted all other ingredients in determining the American class structure. Because there is no such evidence, scenarios about a "custodial state" in which the smart and rich will do everything to protect themselves from the dumb and poor are more the projections of political pundits than they are the conclusions of disinterested social scientists.

Hearts of Darkness

JOHN B. JUDIS

One of the problems reading Charles Murray and the late Richard Herrnstein's *The Bell Curve* is that the authors continually muddy their own water with equivocation, qualification, and even contradiction. Which of these statements do Murray and Herrnstein really believe?

- "We cannot think of any legitimate argument why any encounter between individual whites and blacks need be affected by the knowledge that an aggregate ethnic difference in measured intelligence is genetic rather than environmental."
- "The assumption of genetic cognitive equality among the races has practical consequences."
- "Race is such a difficult concept to employ in the American context. What does it mean to be 'black' in America, in racial terms, when the word black (or African American) can be used for people whose ancestry is more European than African?"
- "It would be disingenuous to leave the racial issue at that. . . . Thus we will eventually comment on cognitive differences among races as they might derive from genetic differences."

Murray has further confused matters by the statements and articles he has written afterwards "clarifying" the book's argument. Murray has insisted, for instance, that the book does not argue for a strategy of eugenics or for strengthening the rule of what they call "a cognitive elite." I would contend, however, that the book's major thrust is exactly this and that the authors' attempts at equivocation and Murray's later attempts at clarification are intended largely to evade

124

responsibility for a thesis that is morally repugnant and scientifically indefensible.

Here is their argument for eugenics. Murray and Herrnstein contend that American blacks and Latinos score on the average significantly lower on IQ tests than whites or Asians do. Lower IQ contributes, they argue, to greater crime, poverty, illegitimacy, welfare dependency, unemployment, and even workplace injury. And because blacks and Latinos reproduce faster and more numerously than whites or Asians do, their proliferation has brought down and will continue to bring down the average IQ of Americans—thereby contributing disproportionately to the country's worst social problems.

To alleviate what the authors call this "dysgenic pressure," they favor eliminating "the extensive network of cash and services for low-income women who have babies" and making "it easy for women to make good of their prior decision not to get pregnant by making available birth control mechanisms that are increasingly flexible, foolproof, inexpensive, and safe." Murray and Hernnstein also recommend that we should alter our immigration policy "to serve America's interests."

Other people, of course, favor these measures for reasons that have nothing to do with eugenics, but what defines a policy is not simply a set of actions, but the intent behind those actions. Only by understanding what is intended can a policy's success or failure be evaluated. Murray and Herrnstein's intent in eliminating welfare payments for the children of low-income women is not to save money or to induce self-reliance among the underclass—the usual conservative rationales—but to discourage the birth of low-IQ children. Similarly, their intent in circulating condoms is not to foster freedom of choice, but to discourage low-IQ women from reproducing. In putting limits on immigration to "serve America's interests," they are not interested in protecting American workers' jobs or preventing an overload of public facilities, but in keeping out people with lower IQs. These happen to be predominately Latinos and blacks who "are, at least in the short run, putting some downward pressure on the distribution of intelligence."

Murray has also denied that he approves of a society stratified according to intelligence, or simply IQ. In speeches, he has assured his fellow conservatives, many of whom fancy themselves to be populists, that he wants to curb the cognitive elite and "return control of daily life to the people who live it." But *The Bell Curve* is a brief for a society divided along exactly these lines. Murray deplores court rulings forbidding the use of IQ tests in hiring. He wants school funds shifted from the "disadvantaged" toward the "gifted." He wants a voucher program that will reward elite private schools. The result of these policies will be still greater segregation of society along the lines of income and of achievement in standardized tests.

Murray describes this society as the "triumph of an American ideal," but it is a perversion of the original American ideal of equality. America's Jeffersonian faith, articulated later by Andrew Jackson and Abraham Lincoln, rested on the ability of ordinary Americans to participate fully in civic and economic life. Jefferson never presumed that all Americans would be entirely equal in income, but he assumed that through the widespread dispersion of property the differences among Americans would not create the kind of invidious distinctions between classes that had ruined Europe.

Murray and Herrnstein do warn against the creation of a "custodial" state in which a cognitive elite attempts to win over and keep in check a growing underclass that reproduces itself through reproducing low IQ scores. But what seems to bother them are not the class distinctions themselves, but the "greater benefits. . . primarily in the form of services rather than cash" that the cognitive elite will bestow upon this miserable mass of misfits. Murray and Herrnstein present two alternatives: a return to an earlier America of neighborhoods and communities (a worthy but probably unrealizable objective) and "dealing with demography"—in other words, discouraging the reproduction of the individuals who require the services of the custodial state. It's eugenics in the service of a racial-intellectual oligarchy.

If these unsavory political recommendations were based on some novel scientific findings, even those who abhor them might have to take them seriously. But Murray and Hernnstein's discussion on race, IQ and dysgenics is not science. It's a combination of bigotry and of metaphysics where, in philosopher Ludwig Wittgenstein's phrase, "language goes on a holiday." Their arguments are sophisticated only in the sense that they repeatedly acknowledge the obvious objections to them. But then they blithely ignore these objections. Let me give two examples:

1. *Correlation and cause:* Murray and Herrnstein acknowledge the difference between demonstrating correlation and proving causation, but consistently use the language of causation when they have merely demonstrated a correlation. They show a statistical correlation between IQ and various social maladies, but they repeatedly describe low IQ as "a factor in," "a significant determinant of," and "a strong precursor of" various social maladies. What emerges is a highly distorted picture of social change. For instance, they ascribe the growing disparity in income to the growing disparity in IQ. But there are other significant factors that have *caused* (and are not merely correlated with) the growing disparity in incomes. These include the decline in unions, competition from low-wage developing countries (which disproportionately affects working-class wages), and, in the case of high CEO salaries, the particularly American identification of income and status. The only evidence that IQ scores have caused the disparity is the correlation itself.

Murray and Herrnstein's confusion of correlations with causes reaches a point of absurdity when they suggest that raising society's average IQ score will reduce crime, unemployment, and poverty. If the average IQ were to rise from 100 to 103, Murray and Herrnstein argue, then "the poverty rate falls by 25 percent... high school dropouts fall by 28 percent... children living without their parents fall by 20 percent... welfare recipiency, both chronic and temporary, falls by 18 percent" and so on! This kind of crackpot utopianism is based upon mistaking a correlation with a cause. It's like arguing that because people with long noses happen to be more intelligent, we could produce a race of geniuses by breeding Pinochios.

Why do erudite members of the cognitive elite make such mistakes? One reason their causal ascriptions seem plausible is that they perform a linguistic sleight of hand on the term "intelligence."

While offering the predictable acknowledgment that "measures of intelligence. . . are a limited tool for deciding what to make of any given individual," they then identify what IQ tests measure with intelligence in the broadest sense, including thoughtfulness, prudence, and wisdom. That makes it easier to attribute a causal role to low and high IQ scores. For instance, after having merely shown that individuals who score poorly on IQ tests are more likely to be unemployed, they conclude that "intelligence and its correlates—maturity, farsightedness, and personal competence—are important in keeping a person employed and in the labor force." Fine—but IQ tests don't measure these qualities.

2. *Race and genes:* The authors also claim agnosticism on the question of whether genes or environment cause low IQ scores, but their analysis is heavily weighted toward genetic causes. They estimate that the genetic component of the difference in IQ between whites and blacks is between 40 and 80 percent, and accept a "middling estimate" of 60 percent, adding that "the balance of the evidence suggests that 60 percent may err on the low side." That's not likely unless the findings of what the authors call the "Jensen School," named after controversial psychologist Arthur Jensen, are given inordinate weight. Indeed, much of the experimental evidence does not support an overwhelmingly genetic view of intelligence.

There is also an underlying logical problem in their argument. Most scientists would agree that the difference in IQ scores between two individuals brought up in apparently similar environments is attributable between 40 and 80 percent to genetic differences. But no test or experiment or finding has ever established that the difference in IQ between groups of dissimilar background and environment are due partly, slightly or primarily to genetic factors. Of course, Murray and Herrnstein acknowledge "that a trait is genetically transmitted in individuals does not mean that group differences in that trait are also genetic in origin." But they then blithely assume that differences in heritability between individuals can be transposed to social groups.

Why would they make such an assumption? It's probably a combination of prejudice, or what they call "underground conviction," and linguistic legerdemain. They acknowledge that neither American blacks nor Latinos represent distinct races, but are a composite of different races, nationalities, and ethnic groups. (The same is equally true of American "whites.") Yet they proceed to describe American blacks as a race and to talk about "genetic differences between the races." By doing this, they impute to the difference between two social groups—American whites and blacks—certain prehistoric genetic traits, making it more plausible to assert that whites are *inherently* smarter than blacks.

While offering their own heinous schemes for raising Americans' "cognitive capital," the authors naturally aver that no necessary conclusions flow from their genetic speculations. "We cannot think of a legitimate argument why any encounter between individual whites and blacks need be affected by the knowledge that an aggregate ethnic difference in measured intelligence is genetic instead of environmental." And on one level, of course, they are right. No necessary conclusions do flow from *their* speculations.

But the last four hundred years provide ample reason to believe that imputing innate inferiority to a group will affect their "encounter" with other groups. In the United States, theories of racial inferiority were the justification for slavery and for restrictions on American immigration. In Europe, for course, these theories were a justification for Nazi genocide. If Murray's and Herrnstein's views gain currency in academic and political circles—and they have already won a warm reception among some conservatives— they will deepen the chasm already separating whites from blacks and Latinos.

Of course, the foresightful Murray and Herrnstein acknowledge that this could occur, but they claim that it is a price we must pay for violating irrational taboos and offending "politically correct public discussion." Let's be clear, however, on what taboo is being violated. It is not some product of Stanley Fish and the academic new left, but of the great war against Nazi Germany. It's not the taboo against unflinching scientific inquiry, but against pseudoscientific racism. Of all the world's taboos, it is the one most deserving of retention.

The "It-Matters-Little" Gambit

MICKEY KAUS

In *Losing Ground*, the 1984 book that made his name, Charles Murray pooh-poohed the role of race in America's social pathology. Instead, Murray blamed liberal welfare programs that trapped black and white alike in poverty. "Focusing on blacks cripples progress," he declared in a 1986 op-ed piece (entitled "Not a Matter of Race"),

> because explanations of the special problems facing blacks nearly all begin with the assumption that blacks are different from everyone else, whether because of racism (as the apologists argue) or because of inherent traits (as the racists argue).

But that was then. Now, it turns out, Murray indeed thinks blacks face problems because they "are different from everyone else," and they are different "because of inherent traits (as the racists argue)" or, at any rate, because of immutable traits. In *The Bell Curve*, Murray and the late Richard Herrnstein contend that blacks have, on average, significantly lower "cognitive ability" than whites, ability that won't be raised in "the foreseeable future." Herrnstein and Murray connect this mental disability with all sorts of pathologies (poverty, crime, illegitimacy). They also use it as the basis for some stark political extrapolations. Affirmative action, of course, must go, since "it has been based on the explicit assumption that ethnic groups do not differ in the abilities" and "that assumption is wrong." For those blacks stuck at the bottom of the bell curve, meanwhile, nothing less than a "custodial state" looms. There is "nothing they can learn that will repay the cost of the teaching." Instead, a "significant part of the population" will be made "permanent wards of the state," subdued and supported in a "high-tech and more lavish version of the Indian reservation."

Let us call this overall argument by Herrnstein and Murray the Ethnic Difference argument. It is but one of several major arguments of *The Bell Curve*, so I should make clear what I'm *not* talking about. I'm not talking about the authors' assertion that general mental ability is in large part genetically inherited by *individuals* from their parents. As Herrnstein and Murray acknowledge, it is one thing to say that differences among individuals are explained by genetic differences; it's something else completely to say that *group* differences are the result of genetic differences rather than differences in the environments different groups face. The example Herrnstein and Murray offer is this:

> Take two handfuls of genetically identical seed corn and plant one handful in Iowa, the other in the Mojave Desert, and let nature (i.e., the environment) take its course. The seed will grow in Iowa, not in the Mojave, and the result will have nothing to do with genetic difference.

Nor is the Ethnic Difference argument implicated in the view, with which Herrnstein has long been associated, that American society is increasingly becoming stratified along lines of inherited mental ability. I have always (perhaps naively) thought this argument of Herrnstein's identified an unfortunate, but real trend.[1] Yet it is a trend that exists quite independent of race; if it is occurring it is occurring among whites as well as blacks, and would indeed be occurring if the United States were composed of a single ethnic group. The Ethnic Difference argument, rather, asserts that blacks disproportionately occupy the lower rungs of this emerging hierarchy by virtue of innate cognitive disability, and they will continue to do so more or less permanently, with the various apocalyptic implications Herrnstein and Murray detail.

Just because many people (myself included) resist this argument as alien and repellent doesn't mean Murray and Herrnstein are wrong. But neither does it mean they are right. Many of *The Bell Curve*'s defenders seem to interpret any disgust with the book as

evidence of a desire to suppress all discussion of the possibility of
ethnic mental differences—to the point where criticism of the book
becomes, in a perverse way, its validation. But the question isn't
whether such ethnic differences in mental ability are possible (it
would be odd if every group averaged the same). The question is
whether Herrnstein and Murray are reliable guides when it comes
to exploring this possibility.

I think not. *The Bell Curve* isn't (as far as I can tell) a dishonest
book, if by dishonesty you mean the falsification of data or the willful failure to recognize unhelpful evidence. But intellectual probity
makes more stringent demands. One is that every assertion be
examined, and reexamined, for its validity. The scholar or social
critic operating in good faith constantly asks himself the question: Is
this really what I think? Is it completely accurate? Or am I saying it
because it sounds good or in some other way serves my own (large,
small, noble, selfish) purpose? It is this test of honesty *The Bell
Curve* fails, at a critical moment.

To make the pessimistic Ethnic Difference argument work, Murray
and Herrnstein must demonstrate three things: 1) that there is a single, general measure of mental ability; 2) that the IQ tests which
purport to measure this ability (and on which blacks score roughly
fifteen points lower than whites) aren't culturally biased; and 3) that
this mental ability is fixed across generations—classically, that it's
"in the genes."

Let us, for purposes of this essay, accept what is in fact quite
controversial: that the first two claims are correct. It's pretty obvious, however, even to a lay reader, that Murray and Herrnstein run
into big difficulties on step three, because it turns out there is a
good deal of evidence that the "B/W difference" in IQ is a function
of environment rather than heredity. There is, for example, the convergence of black and white test scores over the past twenty years,
which Murray and Herrnstein agree has been so fast it is "likely"
due to "environmental changes." There is the "Flynn Effect"—
rapidly rising test scores worldwide. Scores on the Scholastic Aptitude Test, which Herrnstein and Murray say "is partly an
intelligence test," can be increased by over sixty points with less

than 100 hours of studying. French researchers have succeeded in boosting IQ twelve points by placing poor children in affluent homes. IQs were also raised almost eight points by the Abecederian project, which offers intensive day care for five years.

I know of this evidence because it is presented in *The Bell Curve* itself, something the book's defenders regard as a majestic act of evenhandedness.[2] That claim would be more plausible were not these pro-environment findings regarding ethnic differences subjected to a kitchen-sink barrage of objections that have the effect of minimizing their significance—while the pro-genetic evidence, such as it is, receives no such treatment.

In their discussion of the narrowing black-white gap in SAT scores, for example, Murray and Herrnstein admit that if the trend continues, black and white SAT scores would "reach equality sometime in the middle of the twenty-first century." Sounds like the environment may ultimately explain everything! But Herrnstein and Murray immediately suggest that low-IQ black parents are be reproducing at a relatively faster rate, so there is "the possibility that convergence has already stalled." That may be true, but it has nothing to do with the environment versus genes issue, since even if the blacks and white distributions were genetically identical a differentially high low-IQ birth rate among blacks (or whites) would cause their "group" scores to drop. Murray and Herrnstein then toss out a speculative theory that "the convergence of black and white SAT scores... is symptomatic of what happens when education slows down toward the speed of the slowest ship in the convoy." Their scramble to debunk the black-white convergence becomes so embarrassing they insert a defensive note: "Many of you will be wondering why we have felt it necessary to qualify the good news."

And what of the evidence for thinking the difference between whites and blacks is *genetic?* Here Herrnstein and Murray feebly offer "Spearman's hypothesis," which suggests that blacks do worse on questions that tap into general mental ability. But, as the authors admit in the middle of a crucial paragraph, Spearman's hypothesis only suggests the tests aren't biased (i.e., they're really measuring general mental ability). It doesn't mean that the difference in ability the tests measure isn't caused by the environment. I urge a close inspection of this paragraph (page 303, beginning "How does. . ."). It is a wonderful example of how authors can try to conceal a hole in their argument by hiding it in a mess of near-unintelligible verbiage they fervently pray the reader won't bother to untangle. I have written similar fudge-paragraphs myself, but nothing (I hope) as bad as this one.

Even after all this huffing and puffing, the best Herrnstein and Murray can do with the evidence at hand is to declare it "highly likely" that genes have "something" to do with the racial differences.[3] How much? "We are resolutely agnostic on that issue," they say. In other words, the genetic contribution could be 50 percent, it could be 1 percent, or .001 percent, for all they know. Or (though this is not "likely") it could be zero. A significant role for the environment, however, has been substantiated.

Up to this point, Herrnstein and Murray have written what seems to me to be a depressing, but defensible, book. It is not, however, an apocalyptic book. In particular, if (as their own evidence seems to show) genes play a limited role in the black-white difference, there remains substantial hope that by improving the awful environment in which many black children now grow up, America could move the two ethnic bell curves much closer together—close enough, at any rate, for Americans to live comfortably in blissful ignorance of race differences.[4] As Herrnstein and Murray themselves note, referring to their seed-planting example: "The environment for American blacks has been closer to the Mojave."

But this is not the book that Herrnstein and Murray ultimately chose to write. Instead, after twenty tedious pages tendentiously evaluating the evidence on whether the black-white difference is genetic or environmental, they suddenly declare that "it matters little whether the genes are involved at all"![5] If we "knew beyond a shadow of a doubt that all the cognitive differences between races were 100 percent genetic in origin," Herrnstein and Murray declare, "nothing of any significance should change." After all, they argue, what counts in the end isn't the source of IQ differences, but how hard they are to change. And "changing cognitive ability through environmental interventions has proved to be extraordinarily difficult."

In terms of the plan of *The Bell Curve,* this is a dramatic, even brilliant move. The assertion that the gene versus environment debate has no significance—call it the It-Matters-Little (IML) thesis, for short—performs in a single stroke two seemingly contradictory functions. First, it preserves the scary apocalyptic extrapolations at the book's end (the "denouement of our prognosis," in the authors' words). It doesn't matter that the black-white gap may be largely environmental—it will still be immutable, persisting more or less indefinitely, just as if it had been in the genes. The custodial state still looms.

Yet at the same time Herrnstein and Murray defuse the charge (which has come to the mind of any reader of the previous twenty pages) that they believe in *genetic* inferiority. By denying the role of race in *Losing Ground* Murray made himself seem a reasonable, race-neutral scholar. Similarly, by denying the importance of heredity in *The Bell Curve* he and Herrnstein make themselves seem benign, nonracialist fellows even while they predicting more or less permanent black inferiority. It's an impressive feat. No wonder that Herrnstein and Murray said of the IML thesis, in a *New Republic* article published concurrently with the book, that "if we could, we would put it in neon lights."[6]

The only problem with the assertion that "it matters little whether the genes are involved" is that it's crazy. It matters a *lot* if the black-white difference is genetic, because genetic differences in mental ability are almost certainly much harder to alter. Yes, there are simple cures for some hereditary conditions, like baldness. But as yet there is no Rogaine for the brain. Yes, environments are hard to change. They are sometimes passed down from parent to child, just as genes are. But it doesn't follow—and if you read Herrnstein and Murray carefully, they never quite assert—that it would be just as hard to close the black-white gap if it were entirely caused by the environment as it would be to close it if it were based entirely in genetic differences.

The tendency of Murray and Herrnstein to treat Head Start programs—and more limited, intense initiatives such as the Abecederian Project—as if they exhaust the possibilities of environmental intervention is especially disingenuous. First, Head Start and the other projects, as Murray and Herrnstein know, begin after birth. They don't even attempt to alter the prenatal environment, which may be crucial in cognitive development. Second, the Murray of *The Bell Curve* is the same Murray who has suggested (in *Losing Ground* and elsewhere) that by a simple government policy change—ending cash welfare—we could dramatically transform the entire culture in which many young African Americans grow up. Abolishing welfare, Murray has argued, would produce more stable families, more ordered lives, more responsible parents, more law-abiding citizens. Would all this have no effect on prenatal nutrition, or the environment in which children are raised? Murray and Herrnstein assert that "knowing that the differences are 100 percent environmental in origin would not suggest a single program or policy that is not already being tried." Huh? I can name one right off the top of my head: Charles Murray's program.

At a late 1994 symposium on his book, Murray delivered a similar sweeping restatement of the IML thesis, along the lines of "nothing of any significance would change" if genes, not the environment, turned out to be the cause of the black-white gap. What about affirmative action?, someone asked. Wasn't the argument that if blacks were artificially vaulted into the middle class that would change the environment in which the next generation was raised? Doesn't it matter for *that* argument if environment is the key? Gee, Murray responded. He hadn't thought of that example! Yet it's not exactly an obscure one.

Indeed, it's hard to believe that if Murray and Herrnstein had given serious, honest consideration to the IML thesis they would have stuck with it, much less "put it in neon lights." I'm not sure that, even today, if Murray thought seriously about the IML thesis he'd support it. It is transparently indefensible, and the objections to it are hardly ideological. I called up Arthur Jensen, the prominent University of California psychometrician on whom Herrnstein and Murray heavily rely, and asked him if "it mattered" whether the black-white gap was caused by the environment or the genes. "In terms of possible remediation, it would matter a lot," said Jensen, who suspects that prenatal nutrition may play a big role. Jensen was one of the scholars attending the 1994 conference at which Murray made his sweeping IML declaration. He remembers that "the two or three people I talked with believe that Murray was wrong in saying 'it doesn't matter.'"

But of course, if he hadn't said "it doesn't matter" he couldn't have written the dire, paranoid, gripping predictions that now constitute Chapter 21 ("The Way We Are Headed") of *The Bell Curve*. He couldn't have written the jumbled neoconservative rant that fills Chapter 22—or rather, he couldn't have held out the disparate prescriptions in that chapter as the only way to avoid the apocalypse of Chapter 21. Without the IML thesis, his book wouldn't be nearly as "certain to ignite an explosive controversy" (to quote its dust jacket). It also wouldn't sell as well. Rather, Murray and Herrnstein would have had to open the door to all sorts of do-good, liberal, environment-improving initiatives—even affirmative action—as well as tough-minded, conservative, environment-improving initiatives such as welfare reform. "The corn planted in the Mojave Desert that could have flourished if it had been planted in Iowa, wasn't planted in Iowa," Murray and Herrnstein say, attempting (bizarrely) to explain why "it matters little" what caused the black-white IQ gap. Their point seems to be that, whatever the cause, the corn has already failed to grow. But if the cause is environmental, the comeback is obvious: plant the next generation of corn in Iowa. Or water the Mojave.

Am I saying that Murray and Herrnstein consciously embraced a falsehood (the IML thesis) in order to help make their book a best-seller? No. Am I charging that Murray and Herrnstein failed in their elementary duty to rigorously examine the IML thesis because, at least subconsciously, one or both of them suspected that without it the dramatic plan of the book would unravel—and that this central dereliction undermines their credibility as both a scholars and seers? Yes.

NOTES

1. See Mickey Kaus, *The End of Equality* (New York: Basic Books, 1992), 42–48.
2. See, e.g., Daniel Seligman, "Trashing *The Bell Curve*," *National Review,* December 5, 1994, 60.

3.   Richard J. Herrnstein and Charles Murray, *The Bell Curve* (New York: Free Press, 1994), 311.
4.   For the two bell curves see ibid., 279.
5.   Ibid., 312.
6.   Herrnstein and Murray, "Race, Genes, and I.Q.—An Apologia," *The New Republic,* October 31, 1994, 34.

Scientific Truth and the American Dilemma

NATHAN GLAZER

Four years ago, reviewing a major National Academy of Sciences report on the condition of American blacks (*A Common Destiny: Blacks and American Society*, 1989) in *The Public Interest*, Richard Herrnstein laid out the major argument of *The Bell Curve*. *A Common Destiny*, he wrote, "suffers from one crucial failing: it obstinately refuses to consider the evidence concerning racial differences at the individual level." *A Common Destiny* he claimed uses a "discrimination" model to explain differences between blacks and whites in income, earnings, schooling, health, and a host of other factors. He acknowledged that it used no simple discrimination model. Much of what it found could well have been explained by past discrimination, or inadvertent discrimination. (As a member of the committee that produced the report, and an editor of *The Public Interest*, I did not see, as Herrnstein did, a "discrimination" model dominating the report, but he remained firm in his views.) Against this model, Herrnstein proposed what he called a "distributional" model, that is, differences in the distribution of one key trait, intelligence.

To him the difference between the two approaches was stark. But there was after all another kind of "distribution" of blacks, as a result of history, which placed them disproportionately in the South, in the poorer parts of large cities, in occupations that suffered differentially from the impact of economic change. And from these patterns of distribution, consequences could follow that were adverse for blacks, but were neither directly the result of discriminatory actions nor of the "distribution" of intelligence.

Herrnstein gave short shrift to this intermediate approach then, and *The Bell Curve* gives no great weight to it now. Perhaps this approach adopted in *A Common Destiny* could in part be explained by the effort to avoid harsh alternatives. If discrimination was the cause of the miseries of American blacks, then American society stood accused of inherent racism and required further disruptive legal interventions in key spheres of the American economy and society to improve the conditions of blacks. If the "distribution" model explained things, and if one added further, as Herrnstein did, that individual differences in intelligence could not be changed much by environmental influences, then the conclusions were even harsher, but left American society off the hook: Racism and discrimination were not responsible for the black condition, and blacks were doomed to and would have to accept a permanently inferior condition.

But a concern for political implications was not the primary reason for the approach adopted in *A Common Destiny*. I think this intermediate approach, which takes into account a wider range of factors than either discrimination on the one hand or differences of intelligence on the other, is where the weight of the social scientific evidence led the committee. But I will also admit that it is very hard to differentiate in the complex of influences that make for the adoption of a point of view to explain social problems the politically and morally influenced strands from the purely scientific.

I wondered at the time at Herrnstein's description of the key weakness of the report as failing to consider "racial differences at the individual level" (do not such differences aggregate to become group differences?) and at his selection of the term "distributional" to characterize the model he said truly explained black-white differences: I believe in retrospect—sadly, I cannot ask him now—that he was trying to avoid stating in the most direct way (though all the necessary argument was in his article) an explanation of black-white differences that simply leaves men of good will helpless.

There was no reference in this discussion of *A Common Destiny* to a possible genetic basis to explain differences in the distribution of intelligence: the editors of *The Public Interest* would not have allowed it, and Herrnstein at the time probably saw no reason to go into it. But of course it always stood to reason that differences in intelligence, just as many other differences among people, were inborn in some measure, present as part of one's genetic inheritance at birth, and not easily changed over time.

I go into this earlier effort by Herrnstein (there were even earlier ones, of course) to argue the importance of intelligence in understanding individual and group outcomes because I think it throws light on the motivations of the authors. Charles Murray, in his earlier important book, *Losing Ground*, took no account of differences in intelligence: The black condition was the result of misguided social policy, which set incentives which weakened the family and the work ethic among poor people in general, and blacks, because they were disproportionately poor, in particular.

One could see how these two major thrusts to understanding some of our most difficult social problems could be put together. An initial deficit of intelligence placed individuals and groups differently, and because of their different placement they would be affected differently by social policy. The increase in social problems that Murray studied and tried to explain need have no direct connection to any change in intelligence. But Murray's approach was in principle more optimistic than Herrnstein's: Social policy could be changed more rapidly than intelligence. And indeed Murray today plays a major role in arguing for the reversal of the policies that he believes have undermined family connection, marriage, legitimacy, orientation to work, and clearly hopes this reversal will change behavior.

But in *The Bell Curve*, I believe it is fair to say, the pessimistic approach to social policy prevails. The only major policy discussed is affirmative action, and the argument is not that things will be better for blacks if it is abandoned, but that things will be better for the United States if it acknowledges the necessary primacy of merit (that is, intelligence). As for blacks, they will simply have to accept the reality that, being disproportionately placed to the left of the bell curve that describes the normal distribution of intelligence, as a group they will be found less frequently in the occupations based on higher intelligence, more frequently in the low-paying occupations that do not call for high intelligence.

I go into some earlier work by the authors in order to explain motivation: They have been attacked as racists and reactionaries, and the book has been attacked as a social scientific cover for the their prejudices. I think the motivations are very different: They are unhappy at the explanations commonly given for some of the key and most troubling social facts with which we have to deal—the growing inequality in rewards between those who do well in the economy and those who do poorly, and our inability to close the economic gap between blacks and whites. According to this common wisdom, it is the persistent racism of American society, the continuing discrimination against blacks, the selfishness of the prosperous classes and their refusal to be taxed more for social programs and for redistribution of income, that explains the condition of the poor and of poor blacks. No, Herrnstein and Murray say, American society is being given a bum rap, these are not the reasons we have poverty, illegitimacy, crime, dependency, and the like. The reason is the distribution of intelligence, which inevitably means that in a complex society that requires high levels of numeracy and literacy for most economic functions the less intelligent will fall further behind.

I accept and see no good reason to argue with the basic premise in the book: People do differ in intelligence, and many consequences follow. The more intelligent will be better at many things, and will avoid many problems which the less intelligent will not. Nor do I have any argument with the claim that IQ tests (and a good number of similar tests) will give us a pretty good picture of how people differ in intelligence, despite the fact that, following Howard Gardner, one can agree there are other kinds of skills and talents important in explaining how well people will manage in society that are not captured by intelligence tests. Even this much has been found objectionable in the past, and will be found objectionable today. Thus one federal judge in California has ruled, as a matter of law, after trial, that intelligence tests cannot be used to place duller children in classes designed to help them, and intelligence tests have been subjected to massive, book-length assaults by distinguished scientists because some of those who devised and used them believed there were inherited differences in intelligence among races.

More controversial, but also completely convincing to me, is the further claim that there are substantial differences in intelligence among different groups defined by a common experience and a common culture. Yet more controversial, and the principal reason for the assault on the book, is the claim that these differences have their origin not only in environment, experience, culture, but also to some degree in genetic inheritance. Without going into the complexities of sorting out genetic from environmental factors, which are beyond my capacities or knowledge, this does not seem unreasonable to me. The evidence of *The Bell Curve* on these matters may have some problems, but on the basis of a common human experience, which has not yet been shown to be simply nonsense, it stands to reason that there should be some degree of heritability of a trait as important as intelligence, and there could be a number of good biological explanations for differences in intelligence characterizing groups.

Because of what has been made in the past of biological differences, I wish Herrnstein and Murray had pressed further other explanations for these differences among groups before taking up differences in biological inheritance. Indeed, I wish they had dropped resort to such explanations totally: little would have changed in their argument if they had. For the nonbiological explanations will carry us very far, to the point perhaps where we need make no reference to genes at all. For example, we know the income and education of parents positively affects the intelligence of children. If some groups test high in intelligence tests, we often can find explanations in the disproportionate presence of persons of higher education among them. Thus Asian immigrants typically have higher education than the average American. This undoubtedly explains some of their superiority on intelligence tests and in schools. Cultural differences—the intensity of pressure by parents on children to achieve, the willingness of children to dutifully respond to this pressure, greater time spent at homework, and the like—explain a good deal more. Similarly, the urban and commercial background of many Jewish immigrants in the late nineteenth century and early twentieth century compared to the predominantly peasant background of other immigrant groups of the period could explain the higher tested intelligence and greater school achievement of their children.

Herrnstein and Murray could argue that whether they are biological or social, the differences among groups can lead to prejudice, discrimination, and various forms of brutality. Why accept the prevailing aversion to biological explanations? Well, there are very good reasons in recent history for this aversion, and while I would resist a ban on scientific work that tries to trace and estimate biological influences on intelligence, I would still prefer that social scientists press the social side of our explanations before resorting to biology. The latter suggests permanence and unchangeability, certainly in the short run—a few generations at least would be required for change. Certain aspects of culture may be very stable and long-lasting (consider how long groups of Chinese, Indians, and Jews have preserved what I assume to be a culturally based penchant for commerce), but in principle culture can change more rapidly as a result of social intervention than biology. Biology suggests a grim inevitability, and if that inevitability means that blacks will remain in a permanently inferior position in American society, there are good reasons to avoid biology as far as possible. It proposes a quietism regarding our greatest social problem that it would be premature to adopt.

And indeed some of the findings reported by Herrnstein and Murray go against the conclusion of a fixity and unchangeability in intelligence. The National Assessment of Educational Progress has been giving tests in science, mathematics, and reading to groups of schoolchildren of different ages since 1969. The reductions in the differences between white and black performance, in standard deviations, range from .12 to .44. As they write: "The overall average gap of .92 in standard deviation in the 1969–1973 tests had shrunk to .64 standard deviation in 1990. The gap narrowed because black scores rose, not because white scores fell" (p. 291). There has also been a narrowing in SAT scores.

Herrnstein and Murray argue that there are probably limits to this convergence, and perhaps the environmental improvements that have occurred in black living conditions and the reduction in prejudice has already accomplished as much convergence in intelligence-related academic tests as is possible.

Yet one could argue the opposite, too. After all, while we have tried through public policies to do a good deal to raise the educational level of poor children, who are in large measure black, this has not been an overwhelming national effort. Middle-class suburban children generally have more spent on their education in public schools than do inner-city poor children. There has also been a drastic decline in the environment of many of these children—more crime, more drugs, more illegitimacy. While it is not easy to think of ways of reversing these trends, we do keep on trying in scattered and experimental programs, and there is potentially considerable room for improvement in these environmental factors.

One can find other data in *The Bell Curve* that argue against placing too great weight on the biological factor. One of the most intriguing studies referred to in the book compared the children of white and black servicemen and German women. There was no difference in IQ between these two groups of children, a rather surprising result since one would have expected that the half-black children were raised in a less propitious environment (owing to discrimination) than the white children.

Sixty years ago, in their efforts to counter the monstrous racism of the Nazis, social scientists were eager to argue that intelligence can change as a result of environment. That black recruits to the U.S. Army from the North scored higher on intelligence, on the basis of army tests, than blacks from the South, was not too surprising, in view of the huge differences in the schools they attended, but Northern blacks also scored higher, Otto Klineberg argued in *Race Differences*, than whites from the South. There is a good deal to be learned from these regional comparisons, but *The Bell Curve* does not discuss them. Indeed, Klineberg's books do not appear in the massive bibliography.

Should we be talking about genetic factors in differences in intelligence at all? Of course we are talking about them as a result of *The Bell Curve*, and the tenor of the talk, overwhelmingly, is to denounce any suggestion that there might be something to them. The best justification for probing the possible genetic differences in intelligence among races is that this informs us about a truth we should be aware of and whose dimensions we should estimate. I believe it is the search for truth that primarily motivated Herrnstein and Murray. Of course other motives were involved—they always are—and one of them must have been the stubborn insistence on one's right to search for and tell truths against which so many barriers have been erected, not the least of them being the physical danger to the seekers after this truth. The truth has such an unchallenged place in our system of values that once one agrees that what is written is likely to be true, and that it is a result of the search for truth, what more is left to say?

For this kind of truth, one can also however ask, what good will come of it? Of course truth-seekers insist one never knows what good will ensue—the good results will emerge over time, because the truth always produces good, it must. And in any case, the truth is its own reward. We don't ask searchers after the origin of the universe what good it will do. But in this case, I wonder whether we can discern any good results immediately or in the long run. Initially, this truth throws into question (as do other truths on a much less sensational and controversial level, such as evaluations of social programs which show they produce just about none of the results expected) most public efforts to overcome black-white differences.

The Herrnstein-Murray thesis would not necessarily argue against efforts to improve the *education* of blacks: Improvement is possible. The authors note that there is an increase over time in IQ scores generally, owing to environmental changes, but this improvement does not reduce *differences*. IQ scores over time also increase for whites, and this will continue unless one imagines a difference in environmental conditions for educational achievement that so favors blacks and disfavors whites as to keep whites from showing that improvement in scores over time which seems to be common to all. There are perhaps a few cases, in our large cities in particular, in which greater resources, as measured by costs, are put into the education of blacks than whites. But the kind of difference that might help close the gap is hardly imaginable. In any case, that is not the approach favored by the authors. How could one argue that the holding back of improvement in white intelligence so that blacks could catch up is morally legitimate, or would overall improve society? Whites need intelligence, for themselves and for the good of society, as much as blacks.

The authors project an interesting possible utopia in which individuals accept their place in an intellectual pecking order which in large measure affects their income, the quality of their life, their happiness. They are expected to be satisfied with the ordinary pleasures of family, work, community, while others reap the benefits of higher intelligence. It may be true we do not commonly envy the intellectual capacities or accomplishments of others. We allow Einstein and Bobby Fischer their eminence. We can be happy despite the superiority of others at plumbing the mysteries of the universe or playing chess.

But how can a group accept an inferior place in society, even if very good reasons for it are put forth? It cannot. There is a passage on equality by Richard Wollheim and Isaiah Berlin (I take it from Irving Kristol's article, "Equality as an Ideal," in the *International Encyclopedia of the Social Sciences*): "If I have a cake, and there are ten persons among whom I wish to divide it, then if I give exactly one-tenth to each, this will not. . . call for justification; whereas if I depart from this principle of equal division I am expected to produce a special reason." Herrnstein and Murray have a very good "special reason": The smarter people get more and properly deserve more, and if there are more of them in one group than another, so be it. Our society, our polity, our elites, according to Herrnstein and Murray, live with an untruth: That there is no good reason for this inequality, and therefore society is at fault and we must try harder. I ask myself whether the untruth is not better for American society than the truth. Whatever the reasons for the substantial differences in income, living conditions, quality of life between African Americans and other Americans, is it not better for us to act as if public and private efforts, if not those of the past than others that we will devise in the future, can make progress in overcoming them? The evidence is not so fixed, complete, and decisive as to make this an effort in futility.

Equality: An
Endangered Faith

MARTIN PERETZ

Among the classical masters of Yiddish prose, I. L. Peretz, who most readers sadly do not know, also wrote poetry for children. Here is one simple quatrain (roughly translated):

> *Red, yellow, black, white,*
> *Mix the colors up together.*
> *All people are brothers*
> *From one father and one mother.*

It's a variant on Schiller's "Ode to Joy." I first heard it sung by tinny voices to the sonorous choral movement of Beethoven's Ninth. This is what I was taught, and it is what I still believe—not literally, of course, but not just metaphorically either. Men and women of faith take these sentiments more seriously than others in our society, and the erosion of faith, especially among the elites, has certainly sapped the idea of equality of its force as an aspect of creed.

Nothing in my life, however, has ever diminished my experience of essential equality across racial and ethnic lines as both a palpable reality and an unfolding promise. I am a university teacher. Some of my black students have had incandescent minds, and a few were truly brilliant, memorably so. Most were Harvard-smart, like other Harvard students. None was any more unprepared for college work than any other unprepared student. Trying to order my impressions over three decades I find that the intellectual range of black students, from the exceptional to the ordinary, is very much like that of

the range among Jews, other whites, and Asians. But the range at
Harvard and a dozen or so other places is relatively small: theirs are
the advantages of the strong institutions.

The fact is that it is hard to order one's impressions—at least it is
hard for me to do so—by color category because the dynamics of
the classroom are not those of the politics of identity, not even now
in the urgent atmosphere of interracial suspicion so common on the
campus. But we are fast learning, we are being forced to learn, to
see behind every face and behind every phrase the group from
which it emerges. This is a sad development. After all, it was not so
long ago that one's race or religious beliefs or ethnic origins could
fully block even the most remarkable individuals from the paths of
achievement. How many black talents were lost to the commonweal
we will never be able to determine; and, if blacks were not alone in
suffering the burden of their origins at birth, their accumulated suffering and disadvantages were surely more than that of any other
cohort in the population. But inroads were being made against the
received bigotries of the American past. From the early sixties on,
the ascription of in-born virtues and faults to definable groups was
no longer how the culture (and the elite culture in particular)
wanted to do its business. In fact, universities and law firms, hospi-
tals and corporations could no longer afford to recruit with their
own prevailing dominant genealogies as the norm. It was one of the
elevating, albeit short-lived, paradoxes of statist intrusion on civil
society that it insisted—or seemed to insist—that individuals had to
be judged as individuals. As a consequence, a vast democratic revolution took place which even people only in their forties can well
remember: places and positions which previously had been largely
closed to blacks and Jews and Catholics and Asians (and to women,
too) were suddenly open, or much more open. That was the meaning—to take only one small symbolic instance—of the disappear-
ance from college and job applications of the traditional and
all-identifying photograph. Of course, the revolution was not
quickly completed. But it was begun, and America was already a
very different place on account of it.

The Bell Curve would, of course, have been written even had this
departure from democratic norms not occurred. Indeed, research

on intelligence, especially in Britain and the United States, but in the West generally, was central to the meritocratic revolution which unseated static class and ethno-racial strata that had dominated the advanced countries since the beginning of modern times. The attack on intelligence as usable category—and it was a ferocious attack waged over decades—originated in and was supported by these old elites, who were themselves a bit incompetent and a bit inbred besides. The achievement of mobility and fluidity in these societies is, then, directly attributable (although not only) to the routinized use of intelligence testing and of other standard measures in education and employment. That individual capacity would henceforth be the arbiter of individual attainment and reward became the message to the poor and to the excluded (and particularly to immigrants); and it was a welcome message. The work of Charles Murray and Richard Herrnstein stands in this tradition which asserts that individuals are free of the socially ascribed traits of the groups from which they come. If they focused on group profiles of intelligence it is because both law and social policy began to explicitly assume, really for the first time since the Reconstruction amendments to the Constitution, that groups were the salient units of American life. And to the extent that racial and ethnic groups were seen as the salient units so also were their profiles interesting and germane. Doubtless there are still people in the country who resent the mobility of blacks, as before they resented the mobility of Jews. Some of them would have been resentful even if the mobility of all individual blacks was clearly attributable to individual merit. But there is a new norm in place, and it is one that is particularly prevalent where the most coveted prizes of society are being awarded. It is this: the prizes are not only awarded to individuals on the basis of individual qualifications but, when they are awarded to blacks and to members of other designated minority groups, they are awarded as of group right, as an entitlement, to the gifted and the less gifted, equally. In my view, this is a reversal of the democratic revolution on which we had only recently embarked. If anything has put ethnic and racial profiles on everybody's mind it is this departure from what the theory of equality—which was a theory of the equality of individuals—had taught us is just.

Of course, particularly accomplished blacks are the most poignant victims of the new arrangements. Wholly blameless, they fall under a cloud not altogether unlike the cloud which, at some colleges and universities, often hovers over children of the rich and also over athletes. But the regime of racial and ethnic set-asides in education and employment, which is precisely what affirmative action is, makes victims of others who, on simple standards of merit, would have won the places reserved now by custom and law for members of particular groups. We have thus far been spared the historically laden nightmare of having legislatures and courts decide what constitutes membership in these favored groups. Our luck, however, may not hold out much longer. In an economy in which good jobs and generous scholarships are ever scarcer someone will finally have to decide: What constitutes being black? Will one grandparent do?

It may seem churlish to cavil over mechanisms to increase the presence of blacks in areas of the national life where their numbers are proportionally very small. Of course, these mechanisms assume that, were fairness to rule, blacks would be represented at about 10 percent in all of the preferred professions and schools and on the other indices of cultural and economic arrival. But nowhere does life work that way. Were we even to have had a history without slavery the most scrupulously fair distributive patterns of society would have had more scatter-shot and random results than what this notion of representation suggests. There are many discernible groups which are also "underrepresented" in the advantaged places. How many Polish-Americans or Slavic-Americans are there on the faculty of the University of Chicago in a city where their numbers help define the character of urban life? Are there the right number of Irish-descended Americans who are partners in Boston's toney law firms? Are there enough Greek-American Wall Street bankers? Do Norwegian-Americans have their just share of the country's computer scientists? Needn't there be more Arab-American art curators?

These may read like bizarre questions. But they arise with the very logic of the group representation model of society, although these are questions which the model's proponents do not want to answer. This raises another question: Is the model simply a case of special pleading for blacks? If this is not the case and the model works for all, it is burdened by a curious inconsistency in that it makes a fetish of the distinctive life of groups while insisting that these distinctive lives do not incline groups towards different vocational and cultural profiles. Yet where proportionality is the norm it will not long be tenable for half the students at the Julliard School of Music to be of Asian origin. So their surplus numbers will simply have to make way for those who are inadequately represented. And what would be the correct representation of the tens of millions of Americans who haven't the faintest trace of their ethnic past: Are they to be counted under the demeaning rubric of "other"? What an ugly patchwork country we will then be.

There are more or less distinguishing profiles for all groups, and these profiles are expressed in what the groups press on their children. A population which listens to Midori or Itzhak Perlman is likely to produce violinists from among its children, and one that doesn't won't. This is as true for the Irish as it is for blacks. Look around you at any classical music concert or at a museum, and you are seeing why many blacks will not become classical musicians or art connoisseurs. A similar process helps explain why some American ethnicities (like Jews and subcontinent Indians) disproportionally produce physicians and physicists and why others (like Italians and Greeks) also disproportionally produce restaurateurs. I'd be very surprised if these vocational tilts had much of a precise genetic basis. It may be real personal and cultural predilections which have steered these cooks and waiters away from the more brainy professions. And it could also be a consequence of social and economic circumstances. Still, it would be preposterous—wouldn't it?—if we were to establish set-asides in colleges and medical schools and graduate departments of physics (and other sorts of preferences in the ownership of let's say, cyberspace) for Greeks and Italians. But the fact is that society does do all that in behalf of blacks and of a few other stipulated groups. To those groups not similarly favored and also not much numerically present in prestige schools and positions these preferences are especially unfair instances of social engineering. That this social engineering does not actually succeed in producing many more black scientists is scare consolation to those who feel (and are) left out. They begin to think that, if only they'd had the opportunities now widely made available to blacks, they'd be on their way to Nobel prizes.

The black-white differentials in IQ and on other standard measures reassure them in such beliefs. But the black-white dichotomy is itself a coarse division. There is distribution among white ethnic groups as there is among Asians. In America the particular patterns would be hard to reconstruct because ethnicities are so enmeshed and elusive. But if we extrapolated from Europe we'd have some ideas of the statistical distribution of IQ among U.S. whites. Moreover, we do know that on the usual tests of cerebral skills the distribution among American Jews is over the stereotypical top. (Given growing intellectual lassitude among Jews, how long this will be the case is altogether another matter.) But that fact does explain at least some of the black-white difference. If Jews were to be taken out of the white numbers the black-white difference would be smaller. Some white ethnics who may feel a bit triumphant in what they think of as their test-validated sense of group superiority over blacks may be really deluding themselves.

We don't know the exact extent to which mental skills are heritable, and we certainly don't know, to the extent that they are heritable, how they cluster among racial and ethnic groups. But that genetic profiles do cluster among such groups is axiomatic. Professor Samuel Karlin of Stanford has shown in three articles in the *American Journal of Human Genetics* that, in measuring blood protein loci, Ashkenazi, Sephardic, and Iraqi Jews are consistently close in genetic constitution and (where evidence is available) remote from their non-Jewish neighbors. This is true despite the obvious physical differences between the Jewish groups and the virtual visual indistinguishability of these Jews from the people among whom they have lived for centuries. Genetic markers increasingly tell us what groups are prone to what diseases, although, in a lapidary comment, Karlin suggests that " 'Jewish genetic diseases' can be largely an artifact of the intensive data collection among Jewish populations." (But can it be that this propensity has genetic origins?) There is a demography and cartography to genetic markers, the functions of most of which, however, we know little. Still, if science finds the genes determining IQ, it would be very surprising if there weren't some such clustering.

There are many social problems which we seem to lack the imagination to solve, and only one of these is the contagion of ill-functioning black families. These families are not part of the state of nature. Even under the depredations of slavery, we have learned from the work of the late Herbert Guttman, the black family was resilient and protective. Much of this resilience and protectiveness survives, and some of it has been mobilized into the achieving lives of an increasing number of professional, middle class, and working class black families. But here is the rub: the mothers of these functional families are bearing two children, the more achieving the less children, just like among whites. Of course, there are the other mothers, maybe less intelligent, maybe not (and the mostly rogue fathers, most of whom do not work), who produce many more babies who grow up and, in turn, produce still more babies. The fertility rate of American blacks is the highest in the developed world, and this high rate is an expression not of the most competent parents but of the least competent. This is not a happy prospect for anyone. Exodus 1:12 tells us, "the more they were afflicted the more they multiplied." These children needed forty years in the brutal desert before they were ready for ordinary civil life. But the seas will not be parted by Providence, and there is no desert. And, of course, there is no Moses, and there won't be.

Charles Murray thinks that welfare payments are responsible for many of these births which do not augur productive lives, that pregnancy is a Pavlovian response to government money which increases with each newborn baby. Is then, for example, Norplant given to unmarried and unschooled teenagers a wicked eugenic device? Or is it gentle scientific relief for an impulse that ought better be delayed and measured? The nearly 70 percent of black babies born into households without fathers constitutes an American problem from which most Americans are inclined to turn away. But these babies are a demographic problem for blacks who cannot turn away from it, try though some might. (The teenage and nonmarried birth rates are also increasing among American whites and in staid old Europe, too. What we don't know yet is whether the associated pathologies already seen in the inner city will be reproduced in other environments.) We know that, on average, children raised in two-parent families are better prepared for life than those raised in more ramshackle and improvised circumstances. The latter will pull down any and all statistical measure of competence, and real-life measures, as well. They will also be depressed. That's a given. It is also an explanation. Are we past the point of no return? I do not know.

The ingathering of exiles in Israel was not an altogether unprecedented venture. The migrations to the United States also resulted in a grand mixing of different racial types and ethnic histories. This mixing was not nearly so inclusive as it has been in Israel. But its signs are everywhere apparent in our national life. Almost no one is pure anything, and the process continues. When, finally, we are all mixed up together we will be a wiser, warmer, more witty, more lyrical, more beautiful people. And, then, all the standard measurements would be able to tell us about individuals only. God willing, the time is not far off. But God may not have His way.

The Lowerers

LEON WIESELTIER

Charles Murray and Richard J. Herrnstein protest that "the fascination with race, I.Q., and genes is misbegotten," but a few pages later they mutter, about "the environment/genetic debate," that "the question, of course, is fascinating." The question, of course, is not fascinating. It is old, dreary, and indecent, philosophically shabby and politically ugly. The only drollery in Murray and Herrnstein's work is their praise of themselves for their own courage. They seem genuinely to believe that they are going boldly where no man has gone before. A little less statistics and a little more history would show that Murray and Herrnstein are perpetrating, you might say, a rather standard deviation. The Western panic about heterogeneity is ancient, and in its modern versions, in Europe and in America, one of the central representations of this panic has been made by science. Indeed, the "sciences of man" were established in the eighteenth century not least to secure the inequalities and the incongruities of the time with the authority of the natural sciences. Our psychometrically intoxicated conservatives are not the sons of Burke, they are the sons of Buffon (and Taine, and Lombroso, and the awful, impudent, naturalizing rest).

"Here is what we hope will be our contribution to the discussion [of race, I.Q., and genes]," Murray and Herrnstein write. "We put it in italics; if we could, we would put it in neon lights: *the answer doesn't much matter.*" With this, they think that they have acquitted themselves of responsibility for their revival of one of the more deplorable legacies of the Enlightenment. And here is what I hope will be my contribution to the discussion. I put it in italics; if I could, I would put it in neon lights: *their answer doesn't much matter.* For they are still searching furiously for a scientific foundation for

156

generalizations about groups. Murray and Herrnstein may believe that "the fascination with race, I.Q., and genes is misbegotten," but there remains the fascination with race and I.Q., which they have in a bad way begotten; and the latter fascination does not differ in any essential way from the former. Murray and Herrnstein prefer psychological measurements to biological measurements. The inquiry is the same. Only the science is different.

The scientism of Murray (I will not speak of Herrnstein, since Murray is the principal author of the essay in *The New Republic*, "Race, Genes, and I.Q.—An Apologia," to which I principally refer, and *de mortuis nil nisi bonum*) is a little quaint. "The pariah status of intelligence as a construct and I.Q. as its measure," he writes, "for the past three decades has been a function of political fashion, not science." As if it were science that drew Murray to the subject! This distinction between "political fashion" and "science" is too innocent. For the frontiers between the fields are notoriously porous, as the long history of the scientistic study of the races grimly shows. Murray, too, is hiding the hardness of his politics behind the hardness of his science. And his science, for all I know, is soft. You do not have to reject the possibility of certainty in science to reject the certainty of Murray in his science. The occult entity that he calls g is not exactly the sturdy stuff of, say, molecular biology.

Or so I imagine. I am not a scientist. I know nothing about psychometrics. Before Murray, I had never made the acquaintance of "visuospatial abilities" or "the digit span subtest." I do not doubt that there is such a thing as intelligence, and that there are better and worse methods of measuring it. But Murray's enterprise collapses, theoretically and morally, long before he gets to his graphs. For the question of the bearing of science on life is not a scientific question. It is a philosophical question. There is not a graph in the world that will explain the place of graphs in the world.

The belief that the fate of individuals is determined by their membership in a group, however that membership is defined and measured, contradicts the belief that the fate of individuals is determined by the freedom that is the essential characteristic of all individuals, regardless of their membership in a group. There is no way to elide this contradiction. But it is important to be clear about the belief in human freedom. It is *not* a belief in the unconditioned nature of human life. Quite the contrary. It proceeds from a vivid appreciation of the conditions, and proposes that the conditions are not where one ends but where one begins, and that the individual, given the opportunity to make use of powers that he has been given and to come into possession of powers that he has not been given, has the freedom of soul, or mind, or will, to master the conditions, and to deny them the last word about his life.

The belief in freedom recognizes the differences in endowments that distinguish individuals from each other (and those endowments include, obviously, intelligence and membership in a group); the recognition of these inequalities is banal, a common observation of ordinary life. But the belief in freedom, which may be a religious belief or a secular belief, does not quit at the discovery of these inequalities. From its standpoint, rather, it is false to say that all men are equal and it is false to say that all men are not equal. We are, all of us, equal and not equal. We are divided by the specificities of our coming into the world and united by the capacity to neutralize or to modify or to transcend the specificities. We may choose, of course, also to affirm them; but there is no basis in science for such a choice, either. All that science can provide is information about the specificities. The rest is conviction. Empirical inequality cannot erase moral equality. Either you believe in human freedom, and in the universality of human freedom, or you do not. I have no way to judge Murray's statistics, but I have a way (and so does every one of his readers who has made a thoughtful decision about what is possible in human affairs and in America) to judge his view of human agency. It is grossly deterministic and grossly materialistic. In Murray's view of human agency, ought no longer implies can. Can forever dictates ought. To be sure, Murray makes a hasty disclaimer. "This is not to say," he writes at the outset of his essay, "that I.Q. is destiny." But this is followed by his most unattractive euphemism: "In each of these instances, I.Q. is merely a better predictor." Oh, merely.

Here, as elsewhere, Murray offends most when he is trying to be inoffensive. Is it really the purpose of Murray's tome only to find a place for I.Q. on the list of the conditions and the specificities, only to establish intelligence in its relation to race as a variable among variables? Surely Murray's argument is that the explanatory force of this variable is greater than the explanatory force of the other variables, that the influence of the inherited is more formative than the influence of the acquired, that the tangle of the given ("the reality of a difference versus its source") cannot be transcended.

There are, as I say, precedents for this scientistic fatalism. They are not flattering. "All the progress of modern science," wrote Renan in 1854, "leads us to envision each race as confined to a characteristic type that it may or may not achieve, but from which it cannot escape." A few years later Renan wrote about Joseph Salvador, a French scholar of religion who was a descendant of Spanish Jews, that "he brought to his task what we may call an endowment of race, that sort of political insight which has rendered the Semites alone capable of great religious combinations." It will be obvious that this is the sort of philo-Semitic compliment that only an anti-Semite could make.

I am not suggesting, of course, that Murray is an anti-Semite. Still, when I read, on page 275 of *The Bell Curve*, that "Jews–specifically, Ashkenazi Jews of European origins–test higher than any other ethnic group," I am repelled. I am repelled not only because I would like to believe that what I will achieve in my life will be owed to myself and not to my group, though I am honored by my membership in my group; but also because there have been many scientistic comparisons of Jews and non-Jews during the past two centuries in which Jews did not "test higher," and the consequences were catastrophic. What if the "generalizations" that Murray takes from the study that he calls "Storfer 1990" had turned out differently? How would he explain my failure to express the limitations of my group? Or would it be more appropriate, in the event of psychometric embarrassment, that I stop pretending and start tailoring?

These are not unintelligent questions. I am, after all, an Ashkenazi Jew of European origins. More to the point, a retreat to tailoring is precisely what Murray would prescribe for a Jew who discovered, as the result of some new "definitive" measurement, that he was a member of the cognitive underclass. Murray calls his prescription "wise ethnocentrism." It is, essentially, a proposal for pacification. The task, for Murray, is not to teach the low to rise high, since it has been "proven" that they cannot rise high, but to teach the low to find happiness in lowliness. They must learn a strange mixture of resignation and self-love, and abandon any ideal of advancement, and reject all standards of intellectual strenuousness, and subsist in a condition of dreamlessness bordering on mindlessness.

What is keeping the psychometrically disadvantaged down, in Murray's account, is not their psychometric score (or the political manipulation of psychometrics). No, what is keeping them down is their desire to do better. Since they cannot do better, their desire to do better eats away at their self-esteem. They have internalized the standards of others, and so they are judging themselves unfairly. In a fair world, however, inequality would be celebrated. "Given a chance, each clan will add up its accomplishments using its own weighting system, will encounter the world with confidence in its own worth and, most importantly, will be unconcerned about comparing its accomplishments line-by-line with those of any other clan. This is wise ethnocentrism." (Or, as Renan concluded, "the life that disgusts our workers would make a Chinaman or a *fellah* happy. Let everyone do the work he is intended to do, and all will be well.")

It is odd, in this age of ethnic and tribal and racial conflict, for Murray to rhapsodize about "clans" and promote "clannishness" into the source of social peace. But enough theory. "Wise ethnocentrism" is addressed to a particular group in American society: to the blacks, to the stupid and wretched (or rather, the stupid and therefore wretched), "B" in "the B/W difference." African Americans are the ones who must accept the dissociation of fairness from equality. For, as Murray writes moistly, "the experience of slavery perverted and stunted the evolution of the ethnocentric algorithm that American blacks would have developed in the normal course of events." Of course, a stunting of the ethnocentric algorithm of American blacks might also be a result of Murray's racial science; but Murray insists that he is a friend of the losers.

Having delivered African Americans to inferiority and inequality, he tells them to have a nice day, observing sunnily that "the concern about racial inferiority" among American blacks "is diminishing as African Americans define for themselves that mix of qualities that makes the American black clan unique and (appropriately in the eyes of the clan) superior. It emerges in fiction by black authors and by a growing body of work by black scholars. It is also happening in the streets." Why, then, all the melancholy Negroes? That they are dumber should not make them sadder. They may not have a shot at a unified field theory, but they enjoy "the dominance of many black athletes." And that is not all. African Americans differ from "the prevailing Eurocentric model" in many lovely ways. Murray adduces the work of an academic consultant called Wade Boykin to remind us, and more importantly to remind them, that blacks are highly spiritual ("essentially vitalistic rather than mechanistic"), and develop "personal styles" that are distinguished by "verve" and "affect," and share an "emphasis on the importance of movement, rhythm, music, and dance." It is time, he proclaims, to put the rhythm back in algorithm.

Is Murray aware that he has landed himself in the bosom of the most bizarre Afrocentrists? On reflection, though, they deserve each other. They are, all of them, anti-egalitarians and anti-integrationists. They peddle, all of them, cheap stereotypes. They aspire, all of them, to the assurances of biology: the Afrocentrists dabble in melanin and Murray dabbles in genes. They, the Afrocentrists, wish to be done with "the prevailing Eurocentric model," and he, the social scientist confident of having demonstrated that their minds are not designed for "the prevailing Eurocentric model," takes it off their hands. They, fighting the superstition that they are inferior, devise theories of black superiority, and he, peddling the superstition that they are inferior, agrees that they should. What exactly is the difference between the "cultural differences" articulated by Boykin, the educational expert admired by Murray, and the multiculturalist prejudice of the educational expert, cited by Richard Bernstein in *Dictatorship of Virtue*, who maintains that there is an epistemological distinction between Africans and Europeans, since "Africans know through symbols, imagery, and rhythm, while Europeans know through counting and measuring"?

Murray's avenue of approach toward the modern history of

African Americans is utterly unable to account for the rise of a black middle class on the morrow of the civil rights revolution; but he seems altogether aloof from the reality of the people whom he is treating. Thus he remarks about what "is happening in the streets" that it is "normal and healthy." This boosterism about the streets is foolish or wicked. What is happening in the streets, or in an alarming number of them, is not normal and healthy. This is what is happening in the streets: guns, drugs, rape, rats, demagogues, babies, a collapsing pit of dependence and despair.

The village (I mean, the inner city) is burning. And here comes Murray with his blessing. The corollary of his reflections on "the glorious hodgepodge of inequalities of ethnic groups" is complacence: complacence for blacks, since they are denied the ability to intervene in the crisis of black America, and complacence for whites, since they are denied the right to intervene in the crisis of black America. Who are whites to tell blacks that the destruction of families will damage them for an entire era? Don't the bleeding hearts understand that "the mixes are too complex, the metrics are too different, the qualities are too numerous to lend themselves to a weighting scheme that everyone could agree upon"?

Murray's delight in the street betrays also a profound ignorance of African American culture. He reminds me of the rap apologists of the *New York Times*. He, too, wants African Americans to make do with authenticity. He is the hip-hop Herder of the American Enterprise Institute, exalting in the incommensurability of the cultures of America, and warning away the hoary liberals who would judge all the cultures of America by universal notions of truth, goodness, and beauty. And so Murray does not see that he is encouraging the "ethnocentric algorithm" of African Americans in a direction of decline. When Snoop Doggy Dog commands the attention that Johnny Hodges once commanded, there has occurred a decline. When Toni Morrison commands the attention that Ralph Ellison once commanded, there has occurred a decline. And this decline is owed not least to an admiration of the street. As the street rises, the culture falls. Murray is dead to all this. He is just an enemy of promise. After his psychometrics, his lack of pessimism is a little inhumane.

And after his psychometrics, there will be other psychos and other metrics. The panic will not go away; and it is no longer only a panic about heterogeneity. It is also a panic about the futility of social action. The underclass in the inner city may be the first problem in the history of American society toward the solution of which the traditions of American idealism and American ingenuity will avail nothing. A really frightening failure has taken place. The temptation to look upon this development as historically or scientifically inevitable, and therefore to look away, will grow. Murray's work is a surrender to that temptation, and it is not the last one. For this reason, it will be necessary to remind ourselves, again and again, that the differences between values and the differences between groups never coincide; that there is diversity within communities, and not only between communities; that there are human types even as there are racial types, and that all the human types may be found in all the racial types; that all the human types will reach when they think that they can grasp. "When the whole training of life is to make us fighters for the higher," William James wrote angrily on the last page of his copy of Herbert Spencer, "why should it be extraordinary or wrong to protest against a philosophy the acceptance of which is the acceptance of the defeat of the higher?"

Developing the Rage to Win

HUGH PEARSON

In 1966 the civil rights movement segued into the anger-filled Black Power movement and those of us known as Negroes insisted on being known as blacks. We had in mind the complete transformation of what the word means to the nation as a whole. Black Power; Black Is Beautiful; Say It Loud, I'm Black and I'm Proud. These were the campaign slogans designed to assure that the transformation took place. While that may have happened in the hearts and minds of many of us who embrace the word to describe who we are, it never really gained root in the rest of America.

To observe this a person need only look up the word black in *Webster's New World Dictionary,* or any other standard reference dictionary. Besides stating that black classifies a racial group, there is the following: 3) totally without light; in complete darkness; 5) soiled; dirty; 7) evil; wicked; harmful; 8) disgraceful; 9) full of sorrow and suffering; sad; dismal; gloomy; 10) disastrous; 11) sullen or angry [black looks]; 12) without hope [a black culture]; 14) humorous or satirical in a morbid or cynical way [black comedy]. The negative list goes on.

Given that the dictionary is called *New World,* it tells us that nearly thirty years after the black revolution was to have taken place, our "new world" is left with predominantly repulsive definitions of the word. For the most part, the Black Power movement failed. Hindsight has taught us that there were two lasting accomplishments of the 1960s struggle to improve the plight of blacks: the 1964 Civil Rights Act outlawing segregation in public facilities, and the 1965 Voting Rights Act assuring all adult Americans the right to vote. In essence these victories proved we could induce the nation to live up to its constitution, guaranteeing that its legal system would not stand on the side of racism, but no more than that.

That blacks would wish for more out of the movement was understandable. After all, we were far behind everyone else. Though at the beginning of our nation there was some indentured servitude, most immigrants arrived escaping some form of torment or a static society preventing the prosperity they desired. Our African ancestors, on the other hand, arrived for the express purpose of serving as virtual human beasts of burden. After their freedom, blacks became typecast as former slaves, a subgroup which new European arrivals quickly felt better than. Initially such immigrants of the late nineteenth and early twentieth centuries were ranked by the Europeans who preceded them. The Irish, the Poles, Eastern European Jews, and other ethnicities now considered white, were treated as doormats, in some cases experiencing even greater prejudice than former black slaves. Human history has proven that in virtually all large-scale societies, subgroups compete in a struggle, the outcome of which determines which one is to be considered naturally at the top, and which naturally at the bottom.

Eventually blacks became the basement-dwelling caste and the formerly despised European immigrants gained acceptance as whites. The ugly truth that blacks still occupy our nation's bottom social rung is difficult to swallow in our post–civil rights era, since during the turbulent, idealistic 1960s, plenty of Americans were convinced that by the 1990s that would no longer be the case. That we persist in being this in the minds of so many Americans is perhaps best summed up by the racist joke: What do you call a black man with a Ph.D.? Answer: Nigger. This chronic state, along with a rapidly changing economy which has left many unprepared blacks out in the cold, has resulted in a black collective spinning of wheels and a plague of black nihilism in which angry young black males kill one another, produce rap records romanticizing their violent, tough predator images, and reinforce society's fear of black men; poor psychologically defeated blacks care little about their neighborhoods, so graffiti is common, as well as rats and roaches, reinforcing the notion that blacks aren't clean, meaning that even though more than half of black Americans are now middle class, blacks still must fight prejudice when searching for somewhere to live; affirmative action, originally promoted by blacks and whites who considered themselves progressive as a redress for past discrimination, in too many instances lowers standards for blacks in order to fulfill a black quota, thus reinforcing the stereotype that blacks aren't very intelligent.

Then there's the most nihilistic effects of all. A chronic feeling of disconnectedness from the rest of America is so thorough among blacks that large numbers of black youths see no reason to perform well in school. Legions of blacks are so completely consumed by their sense of alienation that they believe Western culture as a whole is white, blinding them to any understanding that they are part of Western culture, which not only originated plenty of breakthroughs but borrowed (and continues to borrow) from a wide variety of other cultures to be what it is.

So when Charles Murray and Richard Herrnstein's book *The Bell Curve* was published in the fall of 1994 and the media immediately zeroed in on its conclusions regarding black intelligence, that amounted to kicking a man while he's down. Though the book is a massive warning about how our nation is rapidly developing a cognitive elite which is increasingly leaving behind a disadvantaged mass of Americans of all colors, blacks feel singled out due to the book's research conclusion that on average blacks of all socioeconomic backgrounds naturally score lower than everyone else on intelligence tests. And a race-weary nation still coming to grips with the failures of the post–civil rights era, finds the bridging of its racial gap rendered even more difficult.

There are any number of ways to debunk *The Bell Curve*'s conclusions. Natural scientists have found absolutely no correlation between race and intelligence. Charles Murray is not a natural scientist, and neither was the recently deceased Herrnstein. The notion that all 30 million blacks constitute a singular race of people, separate and distinct from white Americans is itself a senseless relic of the nation's early history. The vast majority of blacks harbor some degree of European as well as black African ancestry, and 40 percent harbor Native American ancestry too (and some white Americans, southerners in particular, harbor black African ancestry), further complicating any attempt to draw a definitive correlation between race and intelligence.

And why should intelligence be conclusively measured according to such criteria as how quickly a person repeats a sequence of numbers backward, or her or his facility for answering a sequence of multiple choice questions on an exam under time constraints (IQ, scores and SAT scores, among other exams were used by the authors of *The Bell Curve* to draw their conclusions). If such tests are designed purely for the measurement of intelligence, why is a time constraint consisting of a set number of hours even applied to any of the exams, rather than allowing test takers all the time they desire within reasonable limits to complete them? And why are there no essay sections, or fiction and poetry writing elements to assess creativity? It is understandable if a minimum cut off is agreed upon to establish what constitutes normal functioning. But beyond such an assessment why should anyone conclude, with regard to the SAT for example, that a student scoring 500 will undoubtedly contribute less to society than a student scoring 700?

These are all appropriate caveats to *The Bell Curve*'s conclusions. But the danger that they will be used as crutches allowing blacks to continue viewing ourselves as victims, is every bit as great as the danger that publication of *The Bell Curve* provides more comfort to racists. Our tendency to cling to old standards in the way we see ourselves and old solutions to the problems we continue to experience is very great. Thus not only is there a virtual litmus test for deciding who is and who isn't truly black among those most alienated from predominantly white America, there is a virtual litmus test for such a decision among many people who consider themselves liberals and leftists. According to the test, all true blacks must unconditionally support affirmative action in all of its varieties; all true blacks must be Democrats rather than Republicans out of gratitude that the landmark civil rights gains were achieved on the watch of the Democrats; all true blacks must agree that the alarming rate of murder among young black males is due solely to profound changes in our economy, and that any criticism of young black men who murder amounts to blaming the victim and tarnishing the image of all blacks.

Such condescension regarding blacks is so great that it indirectly supports *The Bell Curve*'s implication that blacks are intellectually inferior to everyone else. It implies that responsible behavior, variety of thought and political affiliation, is solely for other people. In other words, our race-obsessed environment has rendered it virtually impossible for anyone black to be an individual in the same manner whites take for granted as their right. Inadvertently our nation has created an environment for being black that imprisons all blacks.

This mental imprisonment all but assures that the definitions for black will remain what they are. In the process blacks are discouraged from learning the lessons other victimized people learned to improve their lot. Such conditioning is furthered by the authors of *The Bell Curve,* not only through the way they use black scores on intelligence tests to imply that blacks are a permanent mental underclass, but in the way they ignored the evidence they uncovered that environment could play the decisive role in blacks catching up to whites on intelligence test performance in the future.

Among their findings was something they called the Flynn Effect, in which over time IQ scores tend to drift upward among groups of people due to environmental improvements overriding any possible genetic basis for IQ performance. Due to the Flynn Effect, average IQ scores among a nation's population have been shown to increase by as much as one point per year, posting gains comparable to the fifteen points separating black and white IQ averages today. Murray and Herrnstein concluded that though the Flynn Effect will certainly increase black IQ averages it won't make any difference in the black/white IQ gap since environmental improvements will also occur among whites.

Such a conclusion is true only if blacks remain imprisoned in the mental environment we find ourselves in. However if we free ourselves from it, there's no question that our individual development on average will post gains at a greater rate then the individual development of our white counterparts so that eventually the black/white IQ gap will be closed.

Freeing ourselves from this imprisonment will entail quite a few mental adjustments. We must overcome our sensitivity to the stereotype that our black African ancestors were savages and that we too, at heart, are savages (which is the foundation both of our insecurity and the persistence of racism). This can only happen if we understand that there are plenty of geographical reasons those black African ancestors never participated in the type of cultural advancement engaged in by their European and Asian counterparts (though there is still much to be proud of with regard to many black African cultures, and there were a few ancient black African civilizations, though eventually they disintegrated).

For instance, as pointed out recently by economist Thomas Sowell in his book *Race and Culture,* unlike Europe, black Africa has no navigable rivers. Also unlike Europe, its coast has no protective ports. In earlier history navigable rivers and protective ports were key to the development of commerce which facilitated the exchange of ideas, the merging of peoples into genuine nations (as opposed to myriad tribes with a multitude of languages which to this day still characterizes black African nations, most of which are simply former European colonies), and the conquering of nations after the development of large naval armadas (by the Spanish, Dutch, English, etc.). Also, our black African ancestors were isolated from other peoples by the massive Sahara desert, which is larger than the entire continental United States.

Furthermore, most of those we now consider white were at one time divisible into northern European barbarians versus people of advanced southern European civilizations (Greece, then Rome). The southern Europeans, in turn, borrowed from the once more-advanced Egyptians and Asians. Northern Europeans only became advanced after being conquered by the Romans. Eventually they learned the lessons the Romans could teach and overtook them, until one day northern Europeans were considered more advanced than their southern counterparts (an image which persists today).

All of this is to say that no group of people has a patent on knowledge. Thus blacks who feel compelled to romanticize black African traditions, many of which amount to barbarism—such as the practice of submitting women to clitorectomies, and the past tradition among a few tribes of killing the wives of the tribal chief upon his death—need not feel compelled to do so just because

racists attempt to disengage blacks from any feeling of connected-
ness with the rest of mankind.

But the most important mental adjustment of all is for each black
individual to decide he or she has no catching up to do in order to
become a complete human being. Not for the purpose of developing a defensive black racism, but in order to muster the self-confi-
dence necessary to meet any challenge, and the desire to allow no
known variety of human knowledge to go unmastered. This is a
type of individual confidence possible only through forgetting *Webster's New World Dictionary*'s definitions of blackness (even if everyone else does not), and through ignoring *The Bell Curve*'s
conclusions about black IQs. We must exchange information with
each other, invite participation from those viewed as nonblack who
genuinely respect us, and meet all challenges with an attitude
exactly like that of a group of junior high school kids in Harlem.

With the coaching of Maurice Ashley, the highest ranking black
chess player in the nation, they were introduced to the intellectual
game of chess.

In earlier times chess was limited to royalty and nobility. Educators have proven that mastery of the game improves abstract thinking skills and thus academic performance. Like high SAT scores
and high IQs, chess mastery generally isn't associated with black
people. But that didn't stop Ashley from accepting the challenge of
teaching the game to the kids. At a recent seminar on chess in education, he recalled, "I went in against the pressure, even of some
educators who felt, why are you teaching these kids chess? And I
really had to be hard on [the kids].... Their attitude was, 'Hey,
you're going to teach us chess? Well we play basketball. Do you
play basketball?'"

Eventually Ashley succeeded in teaching enough of them the
game that they began entering national junior high school chess
tournaments. They called their chess team the Raging Rooks of
Harlem. "We went to our first tournament in 1989. One of our
kids, Michael, lost his first game, and all the other kids won. He was
off by himself, he didn't want to talk about it.... I decided you
couldn't pamper him. When he saw that no one was going to pamper him, he said, 'This is crazy, I have to take this into my own

hands. After that he went five and one. He developed this tremendous will to win. In every succeeding tournament he'd say, 'Come on, we're going to go in there and kick butt!' He came up with all the mottoes for the team. Just before we'd go to play we'd put our hands together and say 'Raging Rooks, yeah!' And Michael would say, 'Well, gotta go to work, gotta go to work,' like it was a business he had to take care of."

The Raging Rooks took care of business so well that two years later they won the National Junior High School Chess Team Championship. Like the Raging Rooks, from here on, not only do African Americans have to hear success is all in the mind, we all have to believe it.

Brave New Right

MICHAEL LIND

The controversy about *The Bell Curve* is not about *The Bell Curve* only. It is about the sudden and astonishing legitimation, by the leading intellectuals and journalists of the mainstream American right, of a body of racialist pseudoscience created over the past several decades by a small group of researchers, most of them subsidized by the hereditarian Pioneer Fund.[1] *The Bell Curve* is a layman's introduction to this material, which had been repudiated by the responsible right for a generation.

Whatever the leaders of mainstream conservatism may claim now, in the seventies and eighties they themselves, and not merely the "politically correct" left, repudiated the kind of arguments that Herrnstein and Murray make. After the civil rights revolution, the mainstream conservative movement, though continuing to engage in covert appeals to racial resentments on the part of white Americans, was more or less successfully purged of the vestiges of pseudoscientific racism (which, it should be recalled, had been just as important as states'-rights arguments in the resistance to desegregation). By the Reagan years, the right, under the influence of neoconservatives in particular, seemed to have permanently rejected its white-supremacist past. With the zeal of recent converts, mainstream conservatives claimed to be defending the ideals of colorblind sixties liberalism, of Martin Luther King, Jr., and Hubert Humphrey, against those who would betray those ideals by promulgating racial quotas and multicultural ideology. Talk of black and Hispanic racial inferiority was relegated to the far-right fringe.

During the entire period that the right was free (temporarily, it now appears) from pseudoscientific racism, there were always a few scholars like Arthur J. Jensen and William Shockley to be found arguing that blacks as a group are intellectually inferior to whites as a group by nature. As far back as 1971, Herrnstein set off a firestorm with his article "IQ" in *The Atlantic Monthly* in December 1971. Much of the dubious research on which *The Bell Curve* rests was accumulated in the seventies and eighties. Why, then, did Herrnstein and Murray—with Philippe Rushton and other neo-hereditarians in their train—take conservatism by storm in 1994, rather than 1984, or 1974? Why are mainstream conservatives suddenly welcoming the revival of eugenic theory, after several decades in which they rejected anything redolent of pseudoscientific racism?

The answer, I would suggest, has less to do with new scholarly support for hereditarianism (there is none) or changes in American society as a whole (it has not changed *that* much) than with the ongoing transformation of the American conservative movement. In a remarkably short period of time, the broadly based, optimistic conservatism of the Reagan years, with its focus on the economy and foreign policy, has given way to a new "culture war" conservatism, obsessed with immigration, race, and sex. This emergent post–cold war right has less to do with the Goldwater-Reagan right than with the older American right of radio priest Father Charles E. Coughlin and the fundamentalist minister Gerald L. K. Smith's Christian Nationalist Crusade. In its apocalyptic style as well as its apocalyptic obsessions, this new conservatism owes more to Pat Robertson and Patrick Buchanan than to William F. Buckley, Jr., and Irving Kristol.[2] The growing importance, within the Republican Party, of the Deep South no doubt also plays a role; Goldwater's and Reagan's Sun Belt conservatism is being rewritten in Southern Gothic style. Race, sex, breeding, class—these are the classic themes of Tidewater reaction.

It is not surprising, then, that long-suppressed ideas about hereditary racial inequality are now reemerging. Their entry, or rather their return, is made easier by the crumbling of taboos that has accompanied the popular backlash against the excesses of political correctness. The nastiest elements on the right now answer any criticism with the charge that they are victims of "PC" (to which the obvious rejoinder is that some targets of the politically correct really *are* racists).

In addition to these general trends, the most important particular factor behind the rehabilitation of pseudoscientific racism on the right may be the recent evolution of the debate among conservatives about race and poverty. For several years a right-wing backlash has been growing against the integrationism and environmentalism not only of liberals but also of certain prominent conservatives. A few years ago, in a perceptive article for *The American Spectator*, the Canadian journalist David Frum identified two schools of thought among conservatives about poverty in general, and black urban poverty in particular. One school, whose major spokesman was Jack Kemp, believed that poor black Americans would respond to the proper economic incentives with entrepreneurial ardor. These conservatives stressed free-market reforms such as "enterprise zones" and the subsidized sale of public housing to its tenants, reforms that, it was claimed, might break underclass dependency on a paternalistic state. The "culturalist" school, identified with thinkers like William Bennett, was more impressed by signs of familial breakdown in the inner city and the perpetuation of a "culture of poverty." The ghetto poor could not be expected to take advantage of new economic opportunities unless their values changed first. When Frum wrote, a third school of pessimistic neo-hereditarians was not engaged in the debate; Kemp and Bennett were both environmentalists, finding the sources of black poverty elsewhere than in the inherited biological traits of poor blacks.

For all their differences, the free-marketeers and culturalists agreed that the problems of the black urban underclass could not be addressed without government activism. In effect, Kemp and Bennett had reasoned their way back to the conclusions of Daniel Patrick Moynihan in 1965 about the need to address the breakdown of the underclass black family by means of substantial social programs. The conservatives who had thought the most about race and poverty were arguing, in effect, for a conservative version of Lyndon Johnson's War on Poverty. Whether it took the form of massive subsidies to public housing tenants or a national network of high-quality orphanages for the children of broken ghetto families (a possibility mooted by political scientist James Q. Wilson), there would have to be government-backed social engineering on a grand scale.

It soon became clear that a conservative war on poverty would be enormously expensive. In the Bush administration, Richard Darman—vilified by the right as a big-spending country-club Republican—actually led the struggle to defeat then Housing Secretary Jack Kemp's proposals for higher spending on the urban poor. As for a national system of quality orphanages and boarding schools, that would cost billions. A call for activist government paid for by higher taxes to help the ghetto poor was not what most conservatives wanted to hear from their experts on urban poverty. The reaction against Kemp's "bleeding-heart, big-government" conservatism on the right was setting in even while he was still George Bush's secretary of Housing and Urban Development. Conservatives who revered the hero of the Kemp-Roth tax cuts began to mutter about the new Kemp, the Kemp who was too eager to embrace big government—and too soft on blacks. The gradual isolation of Kemp within the conservative movement has probably doomed his presidential hopes. The marginalization of Kemp has been most clearly visible in *National Review*, which has criticized Kemp's views on immigration as too soft, and cast him as the defender of the black poor in a strange debate over whether there is a crime problem in America or just a "black crime" problem.

The orphanage proposal has found a proponent in Speaker of the House Newt Gingrich (who in late 1994 hosted a television presentation of *Boys' Town*). The idea probably appeals more to Gingrich, who is fascinated with technological solutions to social problems, than to the resentful voters who put his party into power in Congress. Even Gingrich has not advocated increased *public* funding for orphanages and boarding schools. If he did, Gingrich would probably find himself marginalized within his own party like Kemp.

For all practical purposes, the debate among conservatives about poverty was over before the Herrnstein-Murray controversy even began. Before *The Bell Curve* appeared, and in part thanks to the influence of Murray's earlier book *Losing Ground*, it had become politically impossible for any conservative politician to argue for maintaining current levels of spending on the poor, much less increasing spending. The claim of some conservatives that they merely want to redistribute responsibility between the federal government and the states and private charities is an evasion. Conservatives do not really want states to spend more, in order to compensate for reduced federal spending; they want to slash public spending on poor Americans at all levels. They do not, for example, favor public job creation programs—even at the county level—for poor people thrown off welfare. Furthermore, the claim that private charities will make up for spending cuts ignores the fact that many private charities today receive many of their resources from government. At any rate, if government spending on poor people is demoralizing and encourages addiction and illegitimacy, surely private spending would have the same terrible effects—unless, that is, the parish soup line, that last resort of the destitute, were to be off limits to the children of unwed mothers. In reality most conservatives favor absolute reductions in spending on the poor by public and private agencies at all levels; they are simply not honest enough to say so.[3]

The conservatives, then, agreed on the prescription—reduce or abolish spending on the poor—before they agreed on the diagnosis. The fortuitous appearance of *The Bell Curve* provided conservatives with a useful rationale for a policy of abolishing welfare that they already favored. Had there been no Herrnstein-Murray controversy, the right would still have favored abolishing welfare, but on the familiar grounds that it does not work or backfires by creating perverse incentives. Herrnstein and Murray have provided the right with a new-old argument against welfare which, if it is true, is even more compelling: the underclass (white as well as black) is intellectually deficient by nature, so that ambitious programs to integrate its members into the middle class are almost certainly a waste of money.

This is not the first time that elite Americans have sought to explain the problems of lower-income groups in terms of the allegedly innate biological characteristics of their members. As Dale T. Knobel writes in his study *Paddy and the Republic: Ethnicity and Nationality in Antebellum America* (Wesleyan, 1986):

> During the years immediately before [the Civil War], public officials intent upon uncovering the sources of urban poverty, crime,

and disease, began to recant openly the environmental explanations of social evils accepted for decades and to adopt an "ethno-logic" approach. The Massachussets State Board of Charities insisted that the chief cause of pauperism and public dependency was nothing less than "inherited organic imperfection, vitiated constitution, or *poor stock*," and the New York Association for Improving the Condition of the Poor concluded that "the excess of poverty and crime, also, among the Irish, as compared with the natives of other countries, is a curious fact, worthy of the study of the political economist and the ethnologist. . . ." In 1820 the Irish had only been one of several European immigrant groups regarded suspiciously because of their tutelage under authoritarian political and religious regimes. By 1860, Anglo-Americans had not only separated the Irish out from other immigrants and given them special status as an alien "race" but had also come to treat Irish character as the cause rather than the consequence of their Old World condition.

Now as then, the logic of the hereditarian argument—poverty is caused by genetic inferiority—points toward eugenics programs to discourage the allegedly inferior from reproducing and to encourage fecundity on the part of the allegedly superior. Though Herrnstein and Murray refuse to endorse eugenic measures other than restriction of immigration by persons "with low cognitive ability" and easy access for the poor to contraceptives, others undoubtedly will use their arguments to justify more intrusive eugenic engineering. Already some conservatives have suggested that welfare mothers be temporarily sterilized by Norplant as a condition of receiving relief; the logical next step would be involuntary sterilization of "feeble-minded" blacks, Hispanics, and poor whites, of the kind that was common in the United States throughout most of this century.

It remains to be seen how far the eugenic enthusiasms of the neo-hereditarian right can be taken before they collide with conservative religious convictions. In the early twentieth century, advocates of eugenic sterilization (not only political conservatives, but liberals and socialists) found their most committed adversary in the Catholic church. The employment of a distorted version of Darwinism in the defense of the economic and racial status quo is also problematic in light of the resolute anti-Darwinism of Protestant evangelicals. In the nineteenth century the most radical American racists tended to be secular intellectuals; the biblical account of the common origin and shared opportunity for salvation of mankind prevented devout Protestant conservatives, no matter how bigoted, from treating the different races as separate species or subspecies. In what is surely one of the great ironies of our time, at the end of the twentieth century, as at the end of the nineteenth, the excesses encouraged by eugenic theory in the United States may only be checked within the American conservative movement by the dogmas of resurgent fundamentalism.

NOTES

1. See Lane and Rosen's chapter in this volume.
2. See Michael Lind, "Rev. Robertson's Grand International Conspiracy Theory," *New York Review of Books*, February 2, 1995; Michael Lind, "The Death of Intellectual Conservatism," *Dissent*, Winter 1995.
3. Conservatives in Washington and New York are particularly disingenuous when they claim that the state governments will come up with cures for poverty that have, somehow, escaped the attention of national policy specialists. Who exactly are these untapped policy intellectuals in Sacramento and Austin and Albany who are so much more brilliant than the scholars of the American Enterprise Institute or the Manhattan Institute?

The Phony War

RANDALL KENNEDY

Two broad traditions encompass reflection on the prospects in the United States for racial harmony on the basis of racial equality. One is an optimistic tradition. For example, speaking in May 1865, only five months after the Emancipation Proclamation, Frederick Douglass asked whether "the white and colored people of this country can be blended into a common nationality, and enjoy together. . . under the same flag, the inestimable blessings of life, liberty, and the pursuit of happiness, as neighborly citizens of a common country." He answered "most unhesitatingly": "I believe they can." A century later, Martin Luther King, Jr., also spoke optimistically, declaring on one memorable occasion that he had a dream that the descendants of slaves and slaveholders would one day "sit down together at the table of brotherhood," and announcing in another remarkable speech that he had even glimpsed this promised land of racial justice.

A second tradition is pessimistic. Its central theme is that racial equality in America is an impossibility. Thomas Jefferson voiced this perspective when he stated that it is certain that blacks and whites "can never live in a state of equal freedom under the same Government, so insurmountable are the barriers which nature, habit, and opinion have established between them." Alexis de Tocqueville voiced this perspective too, observing in *Democracy in America* that while he did not believe "that the white and black races will ever live in any country upon an equal footing," he anticipated "the difficulty to be still greater in the United States than elsewhere." He predicted that the lingering consequences of slavery would forever poison race relations here. "Slavery recedes," he maintained, "but the prejudice to which it has given birth is immovable."

The pessimistic perspective is more interesting than its counterpart insofar as it has been voiced by a more ideologically diverse set of people. Some of its adherents have been believers in the inferiority of blacks. Others have been black nationalists like Marcus Garvey and Malcolm X who heatedly deny that blacks are by nature inferior but who also believe that whites are incapable of releasing their belief in and commitment to white supremacy. Arguing in favor of black emigration back to Africa, the black nationalist scholar Edward T. Blyden maintained in 1890 that "it ought to be clear to every thinking and impartial mind that there can never occur in this country an equality, social or political, between whites and blacks." Divided over many things, adherents to the pessimistic interpretation of American race relations share a belief that interracial harmony on the basis of racial equality will never be realized.

The Bell Curve and the controversy surrounding it nourish the pessimistic interpretation. First, and most importantly, the book purports to show that whites are, on average, intellectually superior to blacks not only in terms of present accomplishment but also in terms of future capabilities. Jefferson suspected as much. But Murray-Herrnstein now claim to have proven it scientifically with no recourse to the racist superstitions that have discredited previous assertions of white cognitive superiority. The Murray-Herrnstein presentation of this alleged fact will add a mite of legitimacy to the rumor of inferiority that has loudly echoed for generations throughout American culture.

While the alleged fact of white intellectual superiority does not logically lead to any particular policy prescription, belief in this "fact" has historically prompted or facilitated actions of such devastating divisiveness and degradation that it is no wonder that many observers have doubted the possibility of achieving racial equality in America. After all, among the reasons cited for excluding blacks from the witness stand, the jury pool, the voting booth, and all manner of occupations is that, on average, they are simply too unintelligent to be trusted with performing duties that are best regarded as "white man's business." Given the uses to which claims of racial superiority in intelligence have been put, and the vexed status of the claims themselves, one might have supposed that Murray-Herrnstein would be especially rigorous. Already, however, critics have pointed out Murray-Herrnstein's failure to grapple with the complexities that bedevil "race" and "intelligence," their fundamental terms of reference; their complacent acceptance of tainted, unreliable sources; their overlooking of inconvenient facts; their mischaracterizations of those with whom they disagree; and their apparent ignorance of whole bodies of knowledge relevant to their conclusions.

These very deficiencies signal another reason why *The Bell Curve* and the controversy surrounding it lends credence to a pessimistic interpretation of American race relations. For the book's many evident weaknesses raise the question why it attained the prominence it has received. Some of the contributing causes to the unearned, unwarranted recognition accorded to *The Bell Curve* have nothing to do with the current state of race relations. They stem instead from problems in our intellectual culture that often permit, or even promote, the popularizing of poorly executed books. The biggest problem is reflected by the central, organizing metaphor of our intellectual culture: the *marketplace* of ideas. Popularity, sales, marketing, money, advertising—these are the key words of success in the commerce of books. Sometimes excellence and success in commerce overlap as in the scholarly work of Simon Schama (see, e.g., *Citizens: A Chronicle of the French Revolution*) or James M. McPherson (see, e.g., *Battle Cry of Freedom: The Civil War Era*). But it is precisely the rarity of the overlap that makes such examples so salient.

Given that much of our intellectual life is indeed run as a market, it should come as no surprise that an important reason for the *The Bell Curve*'s success is that Murray-Herrnstein (and their supporting cast of public relations consultants, advertisers, and ideological allies) are good at marketing. Knowing that controversiality attracts attention, they invested heavily into making *The Bell Curve* controversial "news." They did so by loudly proclaiming that the book reveals something hidden and taboo. Hence the publisher's dust jacket proudly asserts that *The Bell Curve* "is certain to ignite an explosive controversy." Many editors, reporters, and TV producers are attracted to this sort of talk. They see controversiality as a good in and of itself. And it probably is for those interested only in selling goods in the cultural marketplace. For those interested in the overall health of our culture, however, the fixation on mere controversiality is a pathology in need of treatment. We ought to distinguish between work that is usefully controversial because it opens up novel avenues of thought and work that is controversial merely because it provides an occasion for shouting about preformed views. The Murray-Herrnstein project falls into the latter category.

The creation of controversiality often involves striking a pose of risk-taking. Murray-Herrnstein do this repeatedly. In an essay published in *The New Republic* (after his co-author's death), Murray claimed that the bigshots with whom they conversed as they researched *The Bell Curve*—"scholars at the top-ranked [of course] universities and think tanks, journalists from the leading [what else?] media, high [not low] public officials, senior [not junior] lawyers, financiers, and corporate executives"—tended to be "scared stiff" about answers to the authors' questions. But Murray-Herrnstein, of course, are not "scared stiff." They fearlessly pursue the Truth no matter where it leads, though interestingly enough it leads unerringly to answers that advance the ideological positions both men have long held. A profile of Murray in *The New York Times Magazine* also shows him cultivating his image as a courageous intellectual. Explaining to the reporter, Jason DeParle, his reasons for writing *The Bell Curve*, Murray is quoted as saying: "Here was a case of stumbling onto a subject that had all the allure of the forbidden. Some of the things we read to do this work, we literally had to hide when we were on planes and trains."

This is an act: the intellectual as Indiana Jones. But the act is a deception. Ensconced at the American Enterprise Institute, feted by *The Wall Street Journal* and *The National Review*, and bankrolled by wealthy supporters of right wing reaction, Murray has little to fear. His views flatter rather than challenge his supporters. Murray's pose reflects on more than just himself; it reflects as well on his appreciative constituency. He would probably drop this pose if a sufficiently large section of his audience demanded that he quit his unbecoming self-congratulatory applause for his own supposed bravery. But the idea of "intellectual courage" has grown quite popular. As frequently used, the term is misleading or inappropriate. First, the people to whom it is applied typically risk little by taking the positions they articulate. In America, controversiality, even utter outrageousness, pays well. Second, the term is inappropriate inasmuch as it fails to illuminate intellectual quality. It might take "courage" for a would-be astronomer to argue that the sun circles the earth. But his willingness to be contentious should not obscure the utter ignorance and erroneousness of his conclusion.

There is another aspect of the pose of courageousness that warrants comment. Murray-Herrnstein inveigh against the alleged "pariah status of intelligence as a construct and IQ as its measure for the past three decades." Their publisher suggests much the same. According to the dust jacket, the authors "break new ground in exploring the ways that low intelligence. . . lies as the root of many of our social problems" and "demonstrate the truth of another taboo fact: that intelligence levels differ among ethnic groups." This is hype. In fact, over a long period of time, a substantial number of investigators have asserted relationships between intelligence and social differences, including racial differences. These data form the basis of the Murray-Herrnstein speculations. But they don't design and conduct experiments and otherwise extract primary information. They leave those chores to obscure, moderately paid academics. Murray-Herrnstein synthesize and repackage this material and bring it to a larger, more lucrative market. Their publisher indirectly acknowledges this on the book's jacket copy. Immediately after proclaiming that *The Bell Curve* demonstrates the taboo "fact" that intelligence levels differ among ethnic groups, the publisher writes that while "this finding is already well-known and widely discussed among psychometricians and other scholars," Murray-Herrnstein "open this body of scholarship to the general public." Contrary to the impression they sometimes give, Murray-Herrnstein are not intellectual pioneers; they are popularizers with a knack for sensationalism.

One must look to more than mere marketing, however, to explain *The Bell Curve*'s prominence. One must also look beyond the possibility that the book's visibility is a function of its intellectual merit, for looked at strictly in terms of intellectual craftsmanship,

The Bell Curve is shoddily constructed. What one must look to are features of our intellectual environment that permit and indeed nurture the success of *The Bell Curve*. The importance of cultural entrepreneurs' hankering for controversiality has already been noted. But to understand what makes the Murray-Herrnstein work a *saleable* controversy requires attention to ugly features of race relations at present. For it is not every controversial utterance that attracts the sort of attention *The Bell Curve* has attracted. Also required are two closely related ingredients that *The Bell Curve* has widely been deemed to have: plausibility and respectability. Much of *The Bell Curve*'s power derives from Murray-Herrnstein's success in tapping into a widespread yearning for explanation and guidance that accepts the claim of cognitive racial inferiority as at least plausible. *The Bell Curve* would not have attracted the attention it has unless the diagnosis it offered was considered to be within the pale of respectable discussion by important arbiters of opinion, e.g., *The New York Times*, *The New Republic*, *Nightline*, etc.

This was best illustrated by the decision of *The New Republic* to print an essay by Charles Murray summarizing the main themes of *The Bell Curve*. Justifying its decision, *The New Republic* wrote that "the notion that there might be resilient ethnic differences in intelligence is not, we believe, an inherently racist belief. It's a empirical hypothesis, which can be examined." The notion that the Holocaust is a lie or greatly exaggerated is also "an empirical hypothesis which can be examined." But one can rest assured that *The New Republic* would have been unwilling to cede any of its pages to Holocaust deniers. It would refuse on several grounds, including the judgment that Holocaust deniers are unworthy of a forum because their claims, like the claim that the earth is flat, has already been decisively refuted. *The New Republic*, however, perceived as open the question of the African American's intellectual inferiority. It is the perceived plausibility of *The Bell Curve*'s racial analysis that prompts arbiters of public opinion to give *The Bell Curve* a hearing. Despite considerable disagreement with it, the notion of black intellectual inferiority is still sufficiently alive to be deemed suitable for serious debate.

The ability of Herrnstein-Murray to reach the highest levels of visibility rests not only on the perceived plausibility of black intellectual inferiority. It rests as well on a willingness by the higher-ups in public opinion management to permit the continued sullying of blacks' racial reputation. Two things in particular contribute to this malign toleration. One is the inability of the black community to discipline effectively those who defame or negligently permit the defamation of African Americans. Notwithstanding all the loose talk about political correctness, it is still largely true that journalists, scholars, and politicians can (and do) show disrespect or even outright antagonism towards blacks without paying much of a price. A second contributing factor also has to do with the convoluted politics of political correctness. Some arbiters of public opinion clearly felt the need to demonstrate publicly that they are not in thrall to PC oversensitivity. To demonstrate independence they joined the pack of journalists whose attention quickly made *The Bell Curve* into a profitable news item.

The Bell Curve controversy nourishes the pessimistic interpretation of American race relations because it elevates to prominence and influence, acclaim and profitability a book whose tone and substance drearily rehashes innuendoes and proposals that should long ago have been consigned to the dustbin of history. At the outset of this century, scholars such as Kelly Miller and W. E. B. Du Bois were forced to write careful refutations of derogatory texts which asserted the racial inferiority of blacks. One assault entitled *The Negro Is a Beast* prompted a response poignantly titled *The Negro Is a Man*. Now, at the close of the century, this struggle continues. It would be a dramatic sign of progress if there existed no felt need to debate Murray-Herrnstein, if one could simply shrug at the *The Bell Curve*'s evident deficiencies, if one did not have to agonize over the dilemma encountered by those who seek, on the one hand, to disinfect this big, sloppy, poisonous book and on the other refrain from honoring it with still more attention. But that is not our present situation. With decisions having already been made to grant *The Bell Curve* tremendous visibility, it must now be debated and refuted and demystified resolutely because its claims, albeit faulty, are nonetheless attractive to influential sectors within American society.

It would be wrong, however, to portray *The Bell Curve* controversy as a reflection of complete stagnation or retrogression in the struggle for racial justice. One of the common deficiencies in recent articulations of the pessimistic interpretation of American race relations is a willful refusal to recognize *dis*continuities as well as continuities in the history of American race relations. The debate surrounding *The Bell Curve*, albeit regrettable in many ways, is nonetheless different from its predecessors. It must be appreciated that Murray-Herrnstein have been met by a quick, vigorous, sustained, and knowledgeable rebuttal. Indeed, the impulse to repudiate *The Bell Curve* is one of the things (among less creditable motivations) that has contributed to the attention it has received. The reaction against *The Bell Curve*, moreover, has not been animated only by liberals or leftists; a significant number of centrists and conservatives have joined in the repudiation as well. While clearly powerful, the cultural-political-social network which loudly and unequivocally champions *The Bell Curve* ethos is by no means ascendant. That is due, in large degree, to effective efforts undertaken by a wide range of people to uproot the racist beliefs, intuitions, and practices that are buried so deeply throughout this culture.

The stigmatization of racism is clearly incomplete. The success of *The Bell Curve* is a dismal testament to that. But the repudiation of *The Bell Curve* and the ongoing dissection of its many failings is also a testament to those strains in American culture which make optimism about the future a sensible alternative.

For Whom the Bell Curves

ORLANDO PATTERSON

1. THE UNDISPUTED FACTS

That there is a significant range of intelligences within the different classes and ethnic subpopulations of the United States, no one would deny. That there is a significant degree of observable average difference in the IQ scores between blacks and whites—one standard deviation to be exact—is also an established fact. That whatever it is that IQ scores measure also correlates significantly with school performance and occupational achievement has been demonstrated. That whites earn more than blacks, have incomparably more political and social power and, in general, enjoy a disproportionately greater share of the economic, social, and cultural resources of the country, is beyond dispute.

That, further, the black population, for two-thirds of its history in the United States—248 of 377 years or .6578 of its history, to be exact—was an enslaved group, physically, economically, socially, legally, sexually, morally, and psychologically, subjected not only to the exploitative whim of individual white owners but at the violent mercy of all whites, and, under the encouragement and protection of the predatory dominant whites, occasionally also of Native Americans—vide the highly developed enslavement of African Americans by the Cherokees—are established historical facts. That among the many net deleterious effects of this experience were not simply their economic and cultural impoverishment, but the destruction of the most fundamental human institution, the family, which was reduced to a reproductive unit denuded of the essential socialization roles of father and husband is, if not beyond argument, fairly established. That, more importantly, and beyond dispute, is the fact that, in evolutionary and comparative terms, the black population has had to struggle for survival under conditions that were unique among modern human populations, possibly all documented human populations: a brutally hostile and unstable environment entailing the periodic mass migrations from kin-based African tribal homeland to transatlantic, highly routinized capitalistic slave system; from the slave system of the old tobacco-based southeast to the slave system of the antebellum southwest; from the postbellum slave compound to serf hovels of the share-cropping system; from post-serfdom rural to the urban south; from farming to marginal industrial economies; from the southern to the northern regions of a vast subcontinent; and from dispersed, low-density fields to hideously congested slum environments. That these monumental changes in environment were encountered, if at all, by European, European-derived, and Asian populations usually over centuries, one at a time—consider the millennium long transition of the European masses from slavery to serfdom to free labor between the sixth and sixteenth centuries A.D.—whereas the black American population was forced to adapt to these changes, sometimes concurrently, over the inhumanly brief period of 37.8 decades. That for all but the last thirty years of their existence after slavery, blacks continued to be subjected to a neodulotic cultural and political environment in which they were systematically terrorized under a lynch regime which not infrequently took the form of collectively organized acts of human sacrifice under the ritual supervision of the professional clergymen of the dominant group; that after being excluded from the agricultural revolution of the southern half of the country by denial of access to its abundant land, they were deliberately shut out of the nation's industrial revolution in its northern half in favor of immigrant whites; that, until 4.1 decades ago, they were excluded from the vastly superior educational and other major cultural resources available to all whites; that, whatever their socioeconomic status, throughout the entire history of their North American ordeal, and to a substantial degree still so, under the all-pervasive ethos of racism, they were, and are, relentlessly and universally propagandized into a sense of their intellectual inferiority and social worth-lessness, socially shunned, mocked in the dominant culture of minstrelsy, debased in the dominant media and literature, dispro-portionately imprisoned and hung, their failures the object of compulsive national prurience (e.g., O.J.; cf. Susan Smith) and collectively despised as physically ugly, morally depraved, and humanly questionable—these are all fully documented historical facts. And there is no parallel in the extant human history of man's inhumanity to man.

The question then is this: What does it all mean? More specifi-cally, what relation do these undeniable facts bear to each other?

2. THE BOOK

My late colleague Professor Herrnstein and his collaborator, Mr. Murray, have amassed the evidence pointing to one simple answer: Spearman's g. Glossing Arthur Jensen, they write: "Once again, the more g-loaded the activity is, the larger the B/W difference is, on average." And what is g?:

> The broadest conception of intelligence is embodied in g. Any-thing other than g is either a narrower cognitive capacity or mea-surement error. Spearman's hypothesis says in effect that as mental measurement focuses most specifically and reliably on g, the observed black-white mean difference in cognitive ability gets larger. At the same time, g or other broad measures of intelligence typically have relatively high levels of heritability.[1]

Let us try to be fair to Herrnstein and Murray, although this is very difficult since they seem to argue for whatever side of the debate suits their purpose. They are not denying the role of envi-ronment, they say. After all, they claim only 60 percent heritability of IQ. And they acknowledge, indeed italicize, a fundamental fact of genetics, namely, that the genetic explanation of within-group vari-ance on a given trait cannot be assumed to apply to its between-group variance. But, typical of their style of argument, they then proceed to cast doubt on just this fact of genetics with a wholly improbable theoretical calculation. If it is supposed that racial differences in intelligence are "solely" due to "some mysterious environmental differences" it would mean that "the mean environment of whites is 1.5 standard deviation better than the mean environment of blacks. . . in percentile terms: the average environment of blacks would have to be at the sixth percentile of the distribution of environments among whites. . . [and] environmental differences of this magnitude are implausible."

This is breathtaking! What does it mean? How can we speak of environmental influences in such terms? Only, of course, residually.[2] We begin by measuring what is presumably measurable, *IQ*. We assume that intelligence is whatever it is that IQ scores measure. We assume, further, that IQ and environment are wholly independent entities and that there is no such thing as an interaction effect between them. We then calculate what the quantitative effect of environment would have to be to account for IQ—the very thing whose significance is being questioned by environmentalists—and we end up with an estimate of environmental effect that is improbable. We therefore conclude that the inference from within group variances must be valid for between group differences. Of course, while boldly stating the implied quantitative environmental effect in their *reductio ad absurdum*, Herrnstein and Murray are careful, at this point, not to state what is also clearly implied, that ergo, heredity accounts for 60 percent of the variance between blacks and whites. This would be asking too much of the readers gullibility given what they had just italicized approvingly. Only later, and gradually, in a method of creeping certitude that pervades the entire book, do we learn that it has been previously established that heritability accounts for 60 percent of the variance between black and white IQ scores. And, in a parallel method of creeping certitude, what had previously been stated with scholarly qualifications—that the magnitude of the IQ test difference between whites and blacks correlate with that of the *g*-loading of the test, whatever *g* may mean—later becomes a proven fact: that the *g*-loading is intelligence and that blacks are genetically endowed, on average, with less of it.

It is not my objective to get into the technical details of *The Bell Curve* in this short article. My motive for the above brief discussion was to illustrate an important aspect of the work: that it is an almost impossible book to come to grips with because of the peculiar way in which materials are used and the argument is expressed. The authors develop their argument in a scattershot way in which all positions and available data are indiscriminately thrown at the reader, including positions that flatly contradict their own. Opposing views are acknowledged, even occasionally applauded, as a way of either appearing to be fair to all sides, or to protect their flanks, but the implications of these opposing views are simply neglected as the authors march on relentlessly to remake their point. On page 310, for example, a major German study of the black and white progeny of World War II GIs which powerfully demonstrates that similar environment leads to the complete obliteration of racial IQ differences, is presented in a little box entitled, "The German Story." It is acknowledged that this study is "certainly consistent with the suggestion that the B/W difference is largely environmental," but there the matter ends. The reader is urged to scratch his head and marvel temporarily as the authors carry on, regardless.

Even more extraordinary, however, are the self-contradictions of which the authors seem blissfully unaware. Thus, we are told on page 297 that "the assumption of genetic cognitive equality among the races has practical consequences that require us to confront the assumption directly," which obviously implies that the assumption or, even more, the demonstration of genetic cognitive inequality among the races has practical consequences. It is with much puzzlement, then, that we read at the end of this same chapter, the author's response to their question: "If it were known that the B/W difference is genetic, would I treat individual blacks differently from the way I would treat them if differences were environmental?" that: **"*We* cannot think of a legitimate argument why any encounter between individual whites and blacks need be affected by the knowledge that an aggregate ethnic difference in measured intelligence is genetic instead of environmental."!** (bold and italics in original) and that the same is true if it were shown that all the differences are environmentally determined. It could be that I am at the far left tail of the IQ distribution and am missing something very subtle and important here, but it seems to me that in this one paragraph the authors have not only betrayed an incredible naivete about the interracial behavior of their fellow white Americans, but have brought into question the whole point of their work.

Other examples abound. A major theme of the book is to bemoan the dumbing down of America and to warn of the rise of a genetically determined meritocracy; and the fifteen point or one standard deviation difference between blacks and whites, not to mention that between the white elite and what Murray elsewhere dismisses as "white trash," are said to be causes for great concern. So it is with much astonishment that we read on page 308 that the fifteen point difference in IQ scores between present-day Americans and their grandparent generation does not necessarily mean that our generation is smarter. Suddenly arguing like environmentalist liberals, the authors blame the inadequacy of the tests for the difference, and, barring that, protect the intellectual and genetic repute of the elite of previous generations by attributing whatever real change the, now questionable, tests imply to an upgrading of the bottom end of the population.

The authors belittle early intervention programs aimed at improving the educational performance of black children, pointing out—as Murray had done in an earlier work—that whatever gains were made, rapidly vanished later in the school lives of these children. It had always struck me, as it has struck others, that the later loss of head-start gains among black children was persuasive proof of the deleterious impact of the environment, in that the more a child was exposed to it, and the less protectively so, the greater the losses to be expected. This is precisely the conclusion reached in a study, ironically by Jensen, which the authors cite, showing that in rural Georgia elder siblings typically have a lower IQ than younger ones and that the greater the age difference between the siblings the greater the IQ differences, and they concur with Jensen that "something" (evidently mysterious and unnameable, but see the second paragraph above) "in the rural Georgia environment was depressing the scores of black children as they grew older" (p. 303). Instead of explaining how this is to be reconciled with their views on remedial programs, the authors proceed to whine about "the asymmetry between the contending parties in the debate." Those who argue for the role of genes, they complain, have never said that the environment does not play a role; only those on the other side arguing for the environment want it all their way in denying any role for genes.

A final example. Herrnstein and Murray in chapter 13 roundly criticize all attempts at cultural and social explanations which employ regression models to control for socioeconomic variables. Controlling for such variables, they note, explains about 37 percent of the original black/white differences in IQ, but they sharply question what is meant by "controlling" for socioeconomic status. The problem, they argue, is that socioeconomic status is itself a function of IQ. People have low status because their parents are genetically stupid and this stupidity is inherited by their children. Controlling for class, or socioeconomic status then, also controls away a good part of the effect of intelligence, which brings the whole procedure into question. The logic is flawless, if one is already persuaded by the genetic viewpoint. However, in the following chapter Herrnstein and Murray proceed to use exactly the same regression models to show how, by controlling for IQ, nearly all the black/white economic differences are explained away, that indeed, blacks end up earning more than whites in professional-technical, clerical, and other occupations. It never occurs to them that the very same logic applies to their own analysis: namely, that someone persuaded by the environmental explanation could similarly contend that, because a good part of IQ differences are class and culturally caused, controlling for IQ entails controlling away a major part of the effects of class and culture.[3]

And so on. I find it hard to take this work seriously. Quite apart from its self-contradictions and the fact that it offers little that is new to the debate, either in the form of new data, or new arguments and interpretations on either side, its mealy mouthed style of discourse is irritating in the extreme: it slinks along, like an irascible, flea-bitten puppy which snaps and bares its teeth one moment even as it prepares to curl its tail and run the next. One longs for the straightforward doggedness, robust scholarship, and honest stance of an Arthur Jensen. It embarrasses me that a Harvard man, whom I knew well and once respected, could engage in such a cowardly discourse.

Alas, one is obliged to take the work seriously. A third of a million Americans—undoubtedly elite and influential Americans, given the price of the book—have bought and continue to buy and presumably read this work. It may well be true too, as the authors claim, that the vast majority of white Americans are already privately persuaded by the view that blacks and the white working classes are genetically inferior and, even worse, that most successful blacks do not deserve their positions, but whites are too intimidated by the ethos of political correctness to admit in public what they sincerely believe in private and whisper among themselves. Not being a white American, I am hardly privy to this simmering undertow of perceived racial injustice and impending majoritarian revolt. If there is any truth to this, however, one had better confront the issues raised by the authors, especially in view of my own belief that much of the current attempt of many black academics and their white liberal supporters to explain the dismal situation of a disproportionate number of blacks in this society is confused and wide of the mark.

3. SOME PERTINENT ISSUES

(I) A GENETIC DETOUR

Let me lead into the few remarks I wish to make by returning to one fundamental issue in the genetics of heredity raised a few years ago by the Berkeley human biologist, Jack R. Vale.[4] The issues concerns the relationship between heredity, intelligence, and the "fitness" of a population for its environment. All biologists agree that intelligence must have been strongly selected for in the evolution of the human species: "human evolution from its inception," writes Vale, "has been shaped by selection for behavioral characteristics, not the least of which is the capacity to comprehend, symbolize, and manipulate the psychological, social, and physical environment. We call this capacity intelligence."[5] The question then arises: Does IQ have anything to do with this view of intelligence. I follow Vale and a significant number of distinguished biologists, including Richard Lewontin,[6] in the view that it has next to nothing to do with intelligence conceived of in this broader, more biologically meaningful way. There is no reason to believe that the capacity to do well at tests under test-taking situations has much to do with an individual or subgroup's ability to manipulate and succeed in its environment.

Ironically, one of the best arguments against the hereditarian approach comes from the genetics of heredity itself.

Heritability (h^2), it will be recalled, is technically defined as the percentage of total phenotypic variance in a given trait which is explained by the genes in question, for a given population. More technically, it is the ratio of the *additive* genetic variance to the phenotypic variance of the trait or character being considered: $h^2 = Vg/Vp$. The fact that it is only the additive variance (Va) which enters the equation must be emphasized, since an important additional fact usually goes unmentioned, especially by psychologists, in discussions of heredity. This is the fact that total genetic variance actually contains two other elements, namely, dominance variance (Vd) and epistatic or genetic interaction variance (Vi). Hence complete genetic variance is properly given by the additive equation: $Vg = Va + Vd + Vi$. Further, taking environment (e) into account, total phenotypic variance on a given trait is $Vp = Vg + Ve$.

Now, recall that, throughout *The Bell Curve*, and indeed among all hereditarian psychologists, it is claimed that intelligence, as measured by IQ tests, is highly hereditary: ranging between .40 and .80, and taken to be .60 by Herrnstein and Murray. If we return to the equation for heredity which is commonly employed—and the one used throughout *The Bell Curve*—($h^2 = Vg/Vp$) in the light of one well established principle of genetic selection, we are immediately faced with what Vale calls a "nice irony." The selection principle in question is the fact that any trait which has been under strong selection for a long evolutionary period will demonstrate very little additive genetic variance and should consist mainly of dominance and possibly epistatic variance, the reason being that almost all the additive genetic variance—which is the only component of the three elements of total genetic variance that responds to evolutionary selection—will have been "used up," so to speak. This being so, the hereditarians are faced with an embarrassing, because inexplicable, dilemma. To quote Vale:

It is true of fitness characters that the proportion of additive genetic variance is small. It is therefore noteworthy that not only the total genetic component of variance (heredity in the broad sense or the degree of genetic determination) of IQ has been found to be so large, but that the proportion of additive variance within that component has been found to contribute the most to it. . . . The question is: If IQ is fitness character, why should the additive variance be anywhere near .71?[7]

Or .60 or .40 or for that matter anywhere other than hovering close to zero, which is where one expects to find the additive genetic variance of a trait that, as the hereditarian psychologists claim, and we fully agree, has been highly selected as an essential factor in the survival and fitness of the human species to its environment.

The problem which Herrnstein, Jensen, and all hereditarian psychologists face then, from the discipline on which they have so heavily drawn, is that IQ scores are *too* hereditary if they are to sustain the claim that these tests have any significance beyond the test center and classroom. Whatever it is that IQ tests are measuring, whatever it is that *g* is—whether it be some Platonic ideal, or *g* for ghost, a pun which Ryle might not have intended when he dismissed the whole thing in his *Concept of Mind* as "the ghost of the machine"—it could have nothing whatever to do with those vitally important behavioral qualities that meaningfully account for our survival in both broad evolutionary and narrower sociological terms.

I return, then, to my more familiar sociological terrain with this understanding of the problem. Intelligence is not an essence but a process, not some operationally inferred static entity, indicated by IQ tests—and the much beloved analogies with the discovery of gravity and electricity are as pretentious and silly as the tautology that intelligence is whatever it is that IQ tests are testing[8]—but that mode of thinking, symbolizing, acting, and interacting which, in their totality, facilitates survival in, and/or mastery of, its environment by an individual or group. It is acknowledged that cognitive functioning is central to this behavioral configuration, and further, that genetic factors are important in its determination—that, indeed, intelligence was a major factor in our evolution as a species—but that there is absolutely no way in which we can meaningfully separate genetic and environmental effects, and that, given the impossibility of conducting experiments on human populations, it is practically impossible, theoretically misguided, sociologically reprehensible, and morally obtuse to attempt to separate or even talk about the two as distinct processes.

Survival in, and mastery of, one's environment are not necessarily any different in the degree of intelligence quotient exhibited when conceived of in these terms, for survival or mastery must always be understood in terms of the challenges posed, or opportunities offered by, the environment. And the environment itself is not a static entity but partly chosen and made by the population in question, which makes the concept of adaptation a discardable tautology, as Richard Lewontin has powerfully argued.[9] The social intelligence demonstrated in the mastery of their environment by a George Washington, Albert Einstein, Charles Darwin, Poincaré, or Colin Powell—all of whom were average to poor students, with Poincaré repeatedly scoring at the level of a moron in all the intelligence tests he took—may be no higher, though more admired, than the social intelligence which is perhaps being exhibited, in gruesome evolutionary terms, by the black underclass. The point is frightening, but has to be made since the discourse initiated by *The Bell Curve* dictates it. If a population is under violent, relentless threat from a dominant, predatory group with whom it shares its environment, if the dominant group after centuries of enslavement, lynchings and brutal oppression and public dishonoring continues to so manipulate the environment that the threatened group has been cornered like rats in blocked sewers which we call ghettoes, if the only options offered by the most powerful leaders of the dominant population is the socially moronic policy, the scorched earth "contract," of more incarceration in already over-filled jails and more state-sanctioned executions in already overcrowded death-rows, then it is both brutally logical, in socioevolutionary terms, and highly intelligent for the threatened group to arm itself to the teeth and behave as murderously threatening and aggressive as it can. It is the same principle that accounts for the survival of hyenas in habitats dominated by lions. It is depressing to have to say it, but had the Jews of interwar Germany possessed one-twentieth of the guns, and exhibited one-tenth of the aggressiveness of the black underclass, six million of them and their descendants would have still been with us, since the cost to the Germans of exterminating them would simply have been too high, as is most certainly true of what it would cost in terms of white lives to get rid of the five to ten million blacks who constitute the despised black underclass. In the light of this horrifying logic, it is no longer clear to me that supporting gun control is a socially intelligent policy for underclass blacks, or for that matter, blacks in general, given the wholly negative and hostile attitude being expressed by the leaders of the dominant group. Herrnstein and Murray may well deny that there is any such implication in their work, but this is typical of their cowardly prevarication, in which what is screamingly obvious from their work is explicitly denied. Every page of *The Bell Curve* points to one inevitable conclusion: that a eugenics policy is the best course of action for dealing with African Americans and the growing "white trash" underclass, and denying this on talk shows in no way alters what the text plainly implies. When we talk or imply eugenics we are in the terrain of evolutionary competition and survival, for we are contemplating a cessation of the most basic evolutionary process—birth. However delicately expressed, however two-facedly denied, such talk amounts to a survival threat, and, in turn, justifies a counter-contemplation of what is most logical and socially intelligent for a group which seeks to ensure its survival.

I do not, let me hasten to add, condone this kind of talk. I find it depressing and dispiriting to have to follow the flow of this particular logic, and in what follows I will be pursuing an entirely different train of thought. But this, I feel obliged to make clear, is one path, the main path, down which *The Bell Curve* leads us.

There are other discursive paths, and to these I now gladly turn.

(II) The Anti-Aristotelian Legacy of the Fathers

Let me first address what, as a historical sociologist, strikes me as one of the most puzzling aspects of the whole IQ controversy. Why is it that, in a land founded on the secular belief that "all are created equal," we are so obsessed with the need to find a scientific basis for human inequality? Now the founding fathers, we have it on Herrnstein and Murray's authority, were very smart men, whatever backward extrapolations one may wish to draw about the revolutionary population as a whole from twentieth-century studies. When they inscribed for eternity in the Declaration of Independence that equality among persons was a self-evident truth, they clearly did not believe that there were no differences between persons. Most of them, certainly Jefferson, had at least a passing acquaintance with Aristotle and would have readily endorsed his view that both the equal treatment of unequals, and the like unequal treatment of equals, were the height of injustice. The Founding Fathers, however, were aware of one cardinal ethical principle guiding social relations which we seem on the verge of abandoning, to our cost. I will return to it shortly.

Clearly, the members of our society differ in a vast number of ways—by gender, by age, by physical prowess, by beauty (more on this later), and most of all by intelligence, understood in the broader sense of capacity to compete and excel in one's society. Some of these differences, at any given time, we regard as very important, others less so, and still others we deliberately choose to disregard. On what basis do we make these decisions? My answer is that there is no known objective criterion for selecting which qualities are important or not. They are always based on value judgments; judgments that are subject to change over time, or even from one part of the country to another.

Now, when the Founding Fathers agreed to the dictum that all are created equal, they were not only encoding a major dictate for the new nation, but, with extraordinary perspicacity, they were implicitly drawing on, and condoning a basic principle of social life. Equality, I am saying, was being proposed as both an end and a means for determining how the new nation was to deal with the problem of differences and of inequality. Their thinking may have gone something like the following. We know, obviously, that there are numerous differences and inequalities among people, and we live by them ourselves; for heaven's sake, we are nearly all major slaveholders! However, we are declaring as an end for the nation the idea that, whatever observable differences there may be between people, it will be accepted that in some fundamental respects they are to be treated as equal: that in the legal and political areas of life people are to be treated as equal, and more generally, that there is an essential core of humanity which, when all differences are shed, we all share, and that in this essential core, we are all to be considered equal. What this is, of course, had to be left vague. It is one of those things which everyone knows, but no one can define, for as Mr. Locke taught us, it is written on the hearts of men. It implies, in a fundamental way, let's face it, that enslavement is wrong, even if there is not much we can do about it for the nation as a whole at the moment. (Actually, Washington the socially smarter, fitter, and morally stronger man, freed his slaves, at great cost to his heirs; Jefferson, the morally weaker man with the greater classroom intelligence and fluency—Boy, and could he write a great line!—did not.)

But equally important is the social principle of action implied by this extraordinary decision to encode equality. It was the implicit recognition of the fact that there are no objective grounds for selecting the ideals we consider important and that therefore there is only one way of doing it: we must arbitrarily chose to do so, based as best we can on our moral principles, and that the way to do it is simply to declare that in this, or that, respect people are to be treated as equal. This same principle of action can be stated in another, deliberately anti-Aristotelian way: namely, equal treatment for equals and unequal in certain specified regards. Or to put it in still simpler terms: whatever distinctions we may observe regarding the trait of interest, we will treat them as socially meaningless. So, for examples, there is great observable inequality in body type and strength, but unequal will be treated equally in this regard; there are great differences between Southerners and Northerners, but the difference will be neglected; there are tremendous differences between Congregationalists, Baptists, and Catholics, and we may be convinced that our faith is superior to theirs, but we will behave as if all faiths are equal in our relations with each other. What about the differences between men and women? In 1787 and for over two centuries thereafter it was agreed that the Aristotelian principle would prevail; they were to be treated differently, and it was an injustice not to do so!

And that between blacks and whites? Here, again, there was little disagreement (as distinct from the distinction between slaves and free, an overlap which confounded the issue, but which nonetheless was made to a surprising degree, many racists being ardent abolitionists): it was an injustice to treat unequal races equally. Even so, the second, equally important aspect of the egalitarian injunction still held in 1787, as it holds today: it was a matter of choice which observable distinctions we choose to make meaningful or choose to neglect. In spite of their abominable "compact of death" with slavery, the Founding Fathers, to their credit, left us with a method of dealing with this and similar differences when the time was ripe or forced upon us.

(III) THE PRINCIPLE OF INFRANGIBILITY

I will briefly discuss three cases of differences which nicely demonstrate the workings of the anti-Aristotelian principle in American life: regional variation in intelligence; age variation in intellectual functioning; and somatic variation in the quality we call beauty. It has long been established that there are significant differences in measured average IQ, as well as performance assessed in terms of, say, contribution to the national income or to the nation's cultural life, between different regions of the country.[10] Whites in Tennessee and rural Georgia score significantly lower than whites in the Northeast, and, on average, live in far worse conditions than their northern counterparts. No one, however, has ever chosen to call the nation's attention to these differences, except in a sympathetic and appropriately sensitive manner. We do not neglect them, but neither do we make a national issue of them, in the process wantonly insulting and dishonoring these people. No one dares to raise the issue of whether or not they are an intellectual drag on the nation; no one bemoans the fact that had they not been a part of the nation our ranking on the international IQ parade would have been much higher. And if anyone—a Charles Murray in search of another hot topic for his next best-selling book—dared to do so, not only is it unlikely that he would find a commercial publisher, it is even less likely that he would find anyone willing to spend over thirty dollars on such a book. Why so? Because whites in Tennessee and rural

Georgia are seen as belonging to the social and moral community which constitutes the American people. Whatever we are, incorporates them. If they are different from northeasterners in one or other respects, the reasoning goes, that is just a fact of our national life, a part of the diverse fabric we take pride in.

Until very recently, there was a consensus among psychologists that intellectual functioning declined with age, especially so after middle age.[11] In this regard, three important changes over recent decades are worth noting. One is the growing size of the population over sixty-five years of age in America. According to the most recent estimate, by 2025 one in five of all Americans will be over sixty-five.[12] With the growing demographic strength of the aged has come their increased political and economic power, the two closely related; it is now established that an extraordinary shift of resources has taken place from the population under twenty-five to that over sixty-five, a shift that continues relentlessly, and is untouchable politically even though it threatens to bankrupt the country within the next quarter of a century.[13] The third major development has been the growing tendency of those over sixty-five to remain in the workplace, reflected most dramatically in the abolition of compulsory ages of retirement.[14] Hence we now face the prospect that one of the fastest growing and most powerful segments of the population—including the working population—is, according to the IQ specialists, an intellectually impaired group with rapidly declining cognitive competence.[15] This, surely, ought to provoke great alarm among those who make it their business to guard the intellectual integrity of the nation. After all, one in five is almost twice as large as 11 percent, which is the menace posed by intellectually inferior blacks; and the aged are growing a lot faster, from all demographic projections. And yet, we have heard almost nothing on this subject from any of those psychologists accustomed to warning the nation about impending psychological and related social disasters. Nor has anyone else chosen to make a crusade of the issue, certainly not in America.[16] No one has made a fortune frightening the nation with apocalyptic forecasts about its impending takeover by an intellectually spent gerontocracy. Why not? For the same reason that we do not engage in public handwringing about the intellectual inferiority of rural white Georgians or Tennesseans. The aged are an integral part of our community; whatever we are as a people, the reasoning goes—and quite rightly I might add—they help to define. If an important and essential part of what we are is in intellectual decline, so are we, and so be it. They are constitutive, and expressions of alarm on the issue, public debate about what to do with them, are egregious and out of bounds, the occasional negative images of aging notwithstanding.[17]

A principle is at work here, one which takes to its sociological conclusion the anti-Aristotelian doctrine of the Founding Fathers. We may call it the principle of infrangibility. It refers to our commitment to a unity which cannot be broken or separated into parts, a commitment to the elements of a moral order and social fabric which is inviolable and cannot be infringed.

And now, to beauty, that "outward gift which is seldom despised, except by those to whom it has been refused," as Gibbon once unkindly put it. We live in what some consider to be a culture obsessed with physical beauty among both men and women.[18] The observable differences are strikingly, and to many, painfully obvious. A few among us are beautiful or handsome, the majority range from attractive to homely to what is considered ugly. What is more, these differences strongly correlate with important indices of psychological and socioeconomic well-being and success. All available studies concur that more attractive persons have much greater self-esteem than others, a pattern reinforced from early childhood. They are perceived as smarter, kinder, healthier, saner, and morally better.[19] Less attractive persons suffer just the opposite set of expectations; indeed, it is well documented that less attractive persons are far more likely to be perceived as mentally unstable and neurologically impaired, even by health professionals.[20] The more attractive also achieve far more in socioeconomic terms, controlling for other factors, and are generally more upwardly mobile than others. Several carefully controlled studies have demonstrated beyond doubt that being perceived as the more beautiful correlates highly with getting the jobs one seeks and the job performance of more attractive tends to be more positively evaluated than less attractive persons.[21] And it has been shown that taller, more handsome presidential candidates nearly always triumph over their shorter competitors.[22] As the short and homely Mike Dukakis learned to his cost, a high IQ, demonstrable managerial competence, and exceptional verbal fluency are no match against a candidate who is tall, handsome, and "classy" looking, however he may mangle the English language every time he speaks. Indeed, it may well be that the beauty quotient correlates more highly with success than IQ, but let us not complicate the issue further. Patzer correctly notes that distinctions of physical attractiveness rank next only to gender and race as easily observable traits on which distinctions are made and he only barely exaggerates in his claim that in many respects distinctions of physical attraction exceed race and gender differences as sources of discrimination.[23]

My point is that here we have a clearly observable pattern of genetically determined differences between persons, correlating highly with social, economic, and psychological achievement, but which we deliberately choose to neglect as an issue for controversy. We nearly all admire and value the quality that beautiful persons have; but at the same time, no one, to the best of my knowledge has ever called for either an aristocracy of the beautiful or for the denigration of those lacking in this quality. To the contrary, we have a well-developed countervalue which condemns any overt expression of favoritism to the beautiful.

Our tolerance for somatic differences is actually highly revealing of many of the more nuanced and complex aspects of our commitment to the anti-Aristotelian egalitarianism inscribed in the Declaration of Independence. And it is especially relevant to that other form of somatic difference among us on which so much heat is generated, the one we call race, so bringing them into relief should be useful. The beauty bias of our society ought to be a matter of great concern to meritocratic psychologists. For, on the one hand, not only is there no known relation between beauty and intelligence—however conceived—but beauty is meritocratically dangerous precisely because it is a trait under strong selection in our society. It was undoubtedly for this reason that Darwin took a keen interest in the subject and called for detailed study of it by social scientists; but not even the great Darwin could get much of a research response, least of all from the hereditarian psychologists who otherwise make so many claims in his name.[24] For all the talk about assortive mating, little account is usually taken of the fact that a disproportionate number of beautiful lower-class women rise up the class ladder each generation by marrying smart, successful men. As Kin Hubbard once observed, "Beauty is only skin deep, but it's a valuable asset if you're poor or haven't any sense."

If the lower class from which these women come is at the bottom of the ladder because its members are stupid—as *The Bell Curve* claims—then untold millions of inferior genes are swarming their way up into the talented classes, dumbing them down. If I am correct, there is no danger in America of our class system hardening into a genetically determined meritocracy.

Sir Cyril Burt once observed that genetic factors were a far better source of mobility in society than environmental ones. Environmental factors easily harden into class prejudice. However, because of the principle of regression to the mean, there will inevitably be a descent of the intellectually inferior members of the ruling class to the bottom and a rise of the smart lower class members to the top. He may well have been right: but only for his native Britain where class prejudices are rigid, people tend to marry assortively within narrow circles, and upwardly mobile members of the lower classes desperately seek wives, whatever their looks, from the higher classes.

The situation is very different in America. There is, to be sure, evidence of a fair level of assortive mating within classes here, but because of the higher volume of mobility, and wider range and fluidity of our classes, there will be tremendous genetic variance even within classes, and if the majority, or even a substantial minority of successful men are choosing their mates on the basis mainly of their looks, the entire meritocratic trend will be confounded, if not aborted. And a good thing too. The enormously successful movie, *Pretty Woman*, should send chills down the spine of every hereditarian.

My point, however, is that Americans generally accept this somatic difference in their population, including all the patently unfair biases in favor of the beautiful as well as its genetic randomization, with equanimity. No one finds these differences and their social consequences disturbing. And no one has ever chosen to make much of an issue of them. Interestingly, one of the most important findings of researchers in this area is the deep reluctance of Americans to acknowledge the role of physical attractiveness in their lives. So entrenched is this denial that social scientists attempting to study the phenomenon often encounter serious noncooperation, including a reluctance of fellow scholars and funding organizations to take the problem seriously. Patzer found that this deliberate "morphology neglect" as one researcher termed it, is invariably attributable "to one of America's most honorable. . . philosophies: *that philosophy being a hesitancy to suggest any form of genetic determinism in the relationship between physical appearance factors and personal characteristics. The sentiment for an egalitarian society has stifled research that may suggest an undemocratic situation in which those persons who possess higher physical attractiveness are, somehow, better than those persons lower in physical attractiveness.*"[25]

"Beauty is not caused," Emily Dickinson once wrote, "it is." As is the difference among us between age groups and the difference between regions; whatever their consequences, they simply are.

Why, we may now ask, does not the same apply to the difference we observe in those somatic traits which together we call race?

(IV) WHOSE DILEMMA?

The simplest answer, of course, is the persistence of racism, both personal and institutional. But this might be too simple an interpretation. There can be no doubt that in many respects personal, or what has been called direct, "dominative" racism has declined substantially in this country. This has been one of the major achievements of the past three decades and the nation can take much pride in this development, especially those blacks, and whites, who struggled and gave their lives for it. Whites in general, too, can take credit for the changes in their racial attitudes, however reluctant they may be to actualize them, a change reflected in any number of surveys, as well as in more in-depth studies. In the simplest terms, one may define the main achievement of the civil rights movement as the forcing upon the nation of the application of the Founding

Fathers' non-Aristotelian method of dealing with differences to the black population. Blacks, in a real sense, are now generally accepted as a constitutive part of the moral order which embraces this great polity.

Indeed, one may go so far as to say that the current obsession with the pathological behavior of the black underclass is a reflection of precisely this new moral inclusion, however vicious the response has been to the new awareness that the behavior some of those whom we have newly come to call our own is unspeakably pathological. It is a paradoxical attribute of human beings that we tend to react more harshly to those to whom we feel a sense of kinship, especially if we feel that the new members of the family have ungratefully betrayed our trust expectations, however unrealistic they might have been.

It is one of the tragic consequences of the unusual oppression of blacks—as is true of all other groups subjected to sustained exploitation—that the oppressed group develops pathological patterns of behavior as one mode of coping, a pathology that victimizes in-group members far more than those of the out-group; in other words, the group becomes its own agent of subjection.[26] As long as they were perceived of as outsiders, such pathologies were matters of little concern to the dominant group: the best nigger, like the best Indian, was a dead nigger, however terminated.

It remains true that fellow blacks are overwhelmingly the victims of pathological members of the population, but with the important difference that the dominant group now seems to care deeply—whatever their politics, and however varied their proposed solutions—about this self-inflicted carnage. It may be a case of spectacular naivete on my part, but this, in my view, is an index of progress in the sense—and only in this sense—that it signals the moral incorporation of black people. The infrangibility principle has, at last, begun to be extended to the group.

If this is true, then we arrive at what must be the most serious criticism of *The Bell Curve:* that in this regard it is a deeply reactionary work, going against the grain of one of the finest traditions of American political and intellectual culture. And to the degree that the kind of thinking, which assumes that blacks remain the quintes-

sential outsiders—natally alienated, social outcasts, the domestic
enemy, the unbeloved, the unfamilial, those who define the bound-
aries of assortive mating, a group whose differences are not to be
treated in the same infrangible way we treat the differences of age
and region and physical beauty, a group whose honor and human
integrity can be violated for a venal sack of royalties—to the degree
that the mode of thinking that undergirds such an exclusion is the
ideological venom otherwise known as racism, that most shameful
grain in the American tradition which the nation has tried so hard,
and so nobly, to overcome in recent years, to that extent is this not
simply a reactionary, but an utterly racist book. It is a charge I do
not make lightly. That it applies in part to a man I knew well, a man
who cared deeply about the genocidal carnage in Europe hardly a
generation ago, a holocaust intellectually supported by this very
same hereditarian ideology, is a cause not only for great sadness,
but for the most pessimistic reflections on the nature of human
nature.

Mention of the pathologies of the black underclass brings me to
my final reflection. When all is said and done, the dreadful statistics
of the black condition in America, of the disparities between the
group and others still confronts us, still needs to be explained.
Something is wrong, horribly wrong, in the condition of one-third
of all black people; and because they are now Americans, in the
urban heart of this greatest of all experiments in pluralistic politics
since the collapse of Rome. At the fragile core of its great urban
centers, embracing the most advanced thought, the richest cultural
life, the most sublime modern architectural structures on the face of
the earth, a people rot in moral and social squalor, nod under the
killing palliative of drugs, wipe each other out for nothing more
consequential than a late-model pair of sneakers, reproduce a generation of malformed, malnourished children, and die the early,
indiscriminate deaths of a late medieval city under plague.

Which takes me back to the second paragraph of this essay.
There can be no doubt that the answer lies somewhere in that inhu-
man record of oppression, the tragic net effect of which has been
that a pattern of behavior emerged in which the group's failures are
now largely self-inflicted. Something is dreadfully wrong with the

culture of black America; we know what its causes were, but to spend more time arguing over who is to be blamed is to blow one's flute while the city burns.

But here we come upon yet another awful contradiction. While black American intellectual leaders, and all those who take a sympathetic interest in the plight of the group, are quick to point to the culturally destructive past as the main source of explanations in defending the public honor, the very humanity, of the group against the onslaught of hereditarians, these very same leaders are equally quick to traduce and vituperate anyone who, in other contexts, dares to point to the cultural deficiencies of the group in trying to explain their condition. It is now wholly incorrect politically to even utter the word culture, as an explanation, in any context other than counterattacks against hereditarians.[27] Indeed so far has this politically correct position gone that it is not uncommon for persons who even tentatively point to social and cultural deficiencies to be labeled and condemned as racists. Consider the intellectual fate of Senator Moynihan.

We cannot have it both ways. If culture is the savior against the hereditarians and those persuaded by *The Bell Curve*, culture must contain the answer as we search for an explanation of the pathological sink into which some 10 million Americans have fallen.

NOTES

1. R. Herrnstein and C. Murray, *The Bell Curve* (New York: Free Press, 1994), 303.

2. It is, of course, possible in experimental situations to make quantitative estimates of environmental determination although, even here, arriving at an estimate of the interactive effect of genotype and environment has proven elusive. See, J. C. Defries, "Quantitative Aspects of Genetics and Environment in the Determination of Behavior," in L. Ehrman et al., eds., *Genetics, Environment, and Behavior* (New York: Academic Press, 1972).

3. This raises the complex issue of how to identify and disentangle social as opposed to natural selection. The two are not mutually exclusive and both kinds of interactions between genetic and envi-

ronmental factors may operate simultaneously. It is difficult sorting these influences out in the experimental study of lab animals; I simply do not see how it will ever be possible to get very far on this score in the study of human populations. Significantly, the experimental studies on mice show that it is precisely with respect to those traits involving a learning component that the genotype-environment interactions are most important. See P. A. Parsons, "Genetic Determination of Behavior (Mice and Men)" in Ehrman et al., 93; and L. Erlenmeyer-Kimling, "Gene-Environment Interactions and the Variability of Behavior," in Ehrman et al., 181–82

4. Jack R. Vale, *Genes, Environment, and Behavior: An Interactionist Approach* (Cambridge: Harper and Row, 1980). I draw, in what follows, especially on chapters 3 and 9.

5. Ibid., 435.

6. Richard Lewontin, "The Fallacy of Biological Determinism," *The Sciences* 116 (2): 6–10.

7. Vale, *Genes, Environment, and Behavior,* 435.

8. Newton did not discover gravity by first cooking up the idea then pestering the world by going on a wild-goose experimental chase after it which successfully terminated with the incontrovertible case of the fateful falling apple. Instead, an incipient theory which had been taking shape for years eventually fell into place, maybe even with the insight from the apocryphal apple, or whatever, and in the light of this completed theory, the existence of gravity was finally understood or "discovered." There is no paradigm, no theory, not even a half-plausible, half-baked notion that begins to explain the mysterious *g*-force cooked up by Mr. Spearman and crystallize into an article of pseudoscientific faith by his disciples. As has frequently been observed, it is possible to make all the claims asserted by the hereditarians—with equal plausibility or lack thereof—without ever eyeing the *g* chimera.

9. See Richard Lewontin, *The Dialectical Biologist.* In this work Lewontin argues persuasively that it is possible to interpret everything of value in Darwinian evolutionary theory without use of the tautologous concept of adaptation, that indeed, the idea was only later adopted by Darwin who, unwisely, came under the influence

of conservative social thinkers—including the reactionary sociologist Herbert Spencer—who found in it, and the related concept of the survival of the fittest (equally irrelevant to the Darwinian theory of selection) a powerful ideological defense of the social horrors of the Victorian capitalist system. Darwin's great contribution to the history of biology is principle of selection.

10. For a recent review of regional differences in test performance see Darrell Bock and Elsie Moore, *Advantage and Disadvantage* (Hillsdale, N.J.: Lawrence Erlbaum, 1986).

11. A classic study claimed that between ages twenty and sixty there was a direct linear decline in intelligence of .3 of a standard deviation or nine IQ points per twenty years. For a review of the evidence see Philip V. E. Vernon, *Intelligence: Heredity and Environment* (New York: W. H. Freeman, 1979), 79–81.

12. George C. Myers, "The Demography of Aging," in R. H. Binslock and L. George, eds., *Handbook of Aging in the Social Sciences* (New York: Academic Press, 1990), 29.

13. According to one estimate, if present trends continue, by 2025 fully 63 percent of the federal budget will be devoted to retirement spending. See G. Hendricks and R. Storey, "Economics of Retirement," in M. Morrison ed., *The Economics of Aging* (New York: Van Nostrand, 1982).

14. On which see E. Howard et al., "Age Discrimination and Mandatory Retirement," in Morrison ed., *Economics of Aging*, 217–46.

15. It should be noted that more recent research has drawn a less pessimistic picture of the decline of cognitive competence among the aged. I find it extremely revealing, and somewhat amusing, that after nearly a century of consensus among psychologists that aging and intellectual impairment are positively and strongly related, psychologists began to change their views on the subject, amounting almost to a volte-face, at exactly the same time that the over–sixty-five segment of the population became large and powerful. Is this merely coincidental? See P. Coleman, "Psychological Aging," in P. Coleman and J. Baird, eds., *Aging in the Twentieth Century* (London: Sage, 1990).

Equally revealing, is the way in which psychologists who work in this area dramatically altered their concept of intelligence so as to facilitate a more favorable and sensitive interpretation of aging, one which protects the honor and intellectual integrity of the aged. We are now, for example, urged to take seriously the distinction between "fluid" and "crystallized," abilities, the latter, based on experience and wisdom, actually growing with age.

Oh that colored folks could command such power and respect! Never mind. See R. B. Cattell, *Abilities: Their Structure, Growth Action* (Boston: Houghton Mifflin, 1971).

16. The situation is different in Britain, where the aged have less respect and there is much talk of "disaster" and "impending crisis," on which see P. Coleman's introduction to his *Aging in the Twentieth Century.*

17. Mike Featherstone and Mike Hepworth have argued that there are persisting negative conceptions of age in the society. Perhaps so, but these in no way vitiate my argument. In a beauty-conscious society such as our own, one would be surprised not to find such negative images. In any case, the way things are going, in terms of the shifting of the nation's resource toward the aged, such carping may soon be the only thing younger people will have left to assuage their penury. See Featherstone and Hepworth, "Images of Ageing," in Coleman and Baird, 250–75.

18. See Gordon L. Patzer's excellent study, *The Physical Attractiveness Phenomenon* (New York: Plenum Press, 1985); and Naomi Wolff, *The Beauty Myth* (New York: Morrow, 1991).

19. K. K. Dion and S. Stein, "Physical Attractiveness and Interpersonal Influence," *Journal of Experimental Social Psychology* 14 (1978), 97–108; and Dion et al., "What Is Beautiful Is Good," *Journal of Personality and Social Psychology* 24 (1972), 285–90.

20. Patzer, 44–46.

21. Ibid., 101–16.

22. R. Keyes, *The Height of Your Life* (Boston: Little, Brown); Patzer, 167–68.

23. Of course, all three can, and often do, overlap, and when they do the effects can be devastating: our by now familiar interaction problem.

24. Charles Darwin, *The Origins of Species by Means of Natural Selection* (1871).

25. Patzer, 6.
26. In this regard, we face the paradox that what circumstances dictate as the most efficient and socially intelligent means of group survival may be in sharp conflict with what is required for optimal survival within that same environment, a contradiction not uncommon in human and non-human populations. Thus the sickle-cell trait may have promoted greater group survival of West Africans in the malaria infested environment, but it may well have reduced their energy level to a degree that prevented optimal exploitation of the otherwise abundant African physical environment. The pathological social behavior of the urban underclass in the face of a social environment infested with racism and a once predatory, and punitive, dominant group may be a tragic social parallel to the sickle-cell trade off.
27. Of course, it is acceptable, indeed, politically most correct, to speak at length of black culture if all we intend to do is praise it.

Contributors

STEVEN FRASER is vice president and executive editor at Basic Books.

HOWARD GARDNER is a professor of education at Harvard University and the author of *Multiple Intelligences*.

HENRY LOUIS GATES, JR., is W. E. B. Du Bois Professor of the Humanities at Harvard University.

NATHAN GLAZER is the author of, most recently, *The Limits of Social Policy*.

STEPHEN JAY GOULD is a professor of geology at Harvard University and the author of *The Mismeasure of Man*.

ANDREW HACKER is a professor of political science at Queen's College and the author of *Black and White*.

JACQUELINE JONES is a professor of history at Brandeis University and the author of *The Dispossessed: America's Underclass from the Civil War to the Present*.

JOHN B. JUDIS is a contributing editor at *The New Republic* and author of *Grand Illusion: Critics and Champions of the American Century*.

MICKEY KAUS is a senior editor at *The New Republic* and the author of *The End of Equality*.

RANDALL KENNEDY is a professor of law at Harvard Law School and the editor of *Reconstruction* magazine.

CHARLES LANE is a senior editor at *The New Republic*.

MICHAEL LIND is a senior editor at *Harper's*.

RICHARD NISBETT is a professor of psychology at the University of Michigan.

ORLANDO PATTERSON is a professor of sociology at Harvard University and the author of *Freedom*.

HUGH PEARSON is an editorial page writer at *The Wall Street Journal* and the author of *Shadow of the Panther: Huey Newton and the Price of Black Power in America.*

MARTIN PERETZ is the editor in chief and chairman of *The New Republic.*

DANTE RAMOS is a reporter-researcher at *The New Republic.*

JEFFREY ROSEN is the legal affairs editor at *The New Republic.*

THOMAS SOWELL is a senior fellow at the Hoover Institute at Stanford University and the author of *Race and Culture.*

LEON WIESELTIER is the literary editor at *The New Republic.*

ALAN WOLFE is the author of *The Human Difference: Animals, Computers and the Necessity of Social Science.*